CW00666038

The German
Offensives of 1918

This book is dedicated to all those on both sides of the wire who had the courage to fight and do their duty in 1918 against extraordinary odds, despite the fear inside them and regardless of loyalties to Emperor or King.

This book is dedicated also to Sally, Joe and Ellie who accommodate my interest and apparently endless talking on the importance of history, military history and 1918 in particular. Thank you all for your patience and amazing resilience.

for

Dear Janet, Annie + Tony –

Campaign Chronicles

The German
Offensives of 1918
The Last Desperate Gamble

Ian Passingham

—◦(◦)◦—

Campaign Chronicles
Series Editor
Christopher Summerville

Enjoy! With much love,

Pen & Sword
MILITARY

9th September 2008

x x x

First published in Great Britain in 2008 by
Pen & Sword Military
an imprint of
Pen & Sword Books Ltd
47 Church Street
Barnsley
South Yorkshire S70 2AS

ISBN 978-1-84415-636-8

A CIP catalogue record for this book is
available from the British Library.

Typeset in Sabon 11/13.5pt by
Concept, Huddersfield

Printed and bound in England by
Biddles Ltd

Pen & Sword Books Ltd incorporates the imprints of Pen & Sword
Aviation, Pen & Sword Maritime, Pen & Sword Military, Wharncliffe
Local History, Pen and Sword Select, Pen and Sword Military Classics
and Leo Cooper.

For a complete list of Pen & Sword titles please contact
PEN & SWORD BOOKS LIMITED
47 Church Street, Barnsley, South Yorkshire, S70 2AS, England
E-mail: enquiries@pen-and-sword.co.uk
Website: www.pen-and-sword.co.uk

Contents

List of Illustrations and Maps

———— ►(•)◄ ————

Illustrations

'Kaiser Bill', von Hindenburg and Crown Prince 'Willy'.
FM Sir Douglas Haig.
Young German recruits in 1917.
British soldier: Eighteen in 1918.
American Troops Arrive in France in 1917.
American prisoners 'at the Kaiser's pleasure'.
British Mark IV Tank.
German A7V Tank.
Stormtroops.
A typical German Stormtrooper.
Salvation Army girls making pies for the boys in the front line.
WAACs tending graves at Abbeville, February 1918.
FM Paul von Hindenburg and General Erich Ludendorff.
'Happy New Year', Christmas 1917, *Die Notenkraker*, 22 December 1917.
Operation Michael: German artillery unit moves through St Quentin, 21 March 1918.
British prisoners of war, March 1918.
Anglo-French co-operation, March 1918.
'Killed in Action' by German artist Kathe Kollwitz.
German Machine-Gun crew, 1918.
A German soldier provides some comfort for a wounded British prisoner.

The German Offensives of 1918

List of Illustrations and Maps

Poignant image: German machine-gunner killed in the last week of the war.

Arrival of the first German military trains. Home – and for good – November 1918.

German troops return to the Fatherland, November 1918.

Maps

1. The Western Front: Showing Allied Gains in 1916 and 1917
2. German Offensives 1918: Front Line on 20 March and Subsequent German Gains From 21 March to 17 July
3. Situation at the End of 1918: Showing the Limits of the German Advance and the Subsequent Allied Counter-Offensive

Maps

The Western Front
Showing Allied Gains in 1916 and 1917
- - - - Hindenburg Line ━━━ Approx. Front Line 1916

0   20   40
Miles

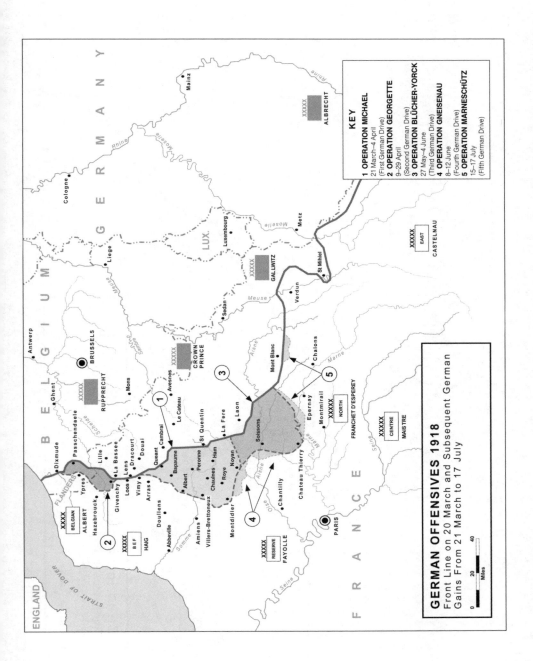

GERMAN OFFENSIVES 1918

Front Line on 20 March and Subsequent German
Gains From 21 March to 17 July

KEY

1 OPERATION MICHAEL
21 March–4 April
(First German Drive)

2 OPERATION GEORGETTE
9–29 April
(Second German Drive)

3 OPERATION BLÜCHER-YORCK
27 May–4 June
(Third German Drive)

4 OPERATION GNEISENAU
8–12 June
(Fourth German Drive)

5 OPERATION MARNESCHÜTZ
15–17 July
(Fifth German Drive)

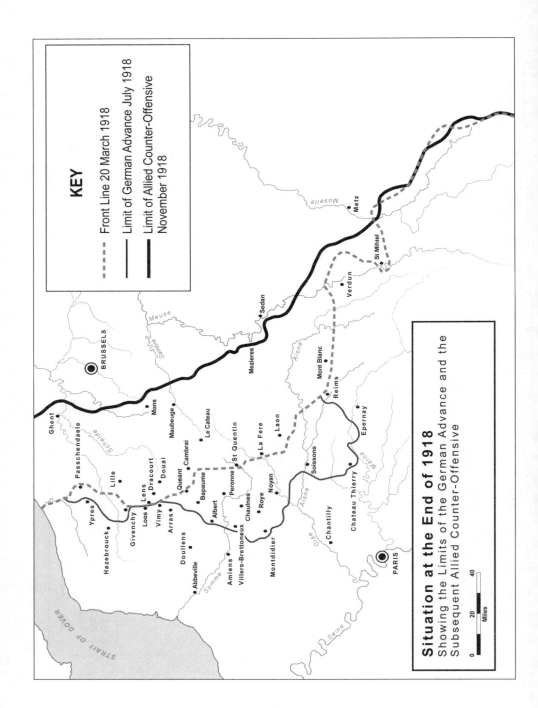

KEY

- - - - Front Line 20 March 1918
——— Limit of German Advance July 1918
━━━━ Limit of Allied Counter-Offensive
November 1918

Situation at the End of 1918

Showing the Limits of the German Advance and the Subsequent Allied Counter-Offensive

0   20   40
Miles

STRAIT OF DOVER

Ghent
Passchendaele
Ypres
Hazebrouck
Lille
Givenchy
Loos Lens
Vimy
Abbeville
Doullens
Arras
Amiens
Villers-Brettoneux
Albert
Bapaume
Montdidier
Chaulnes
Roye
Peronne
Noyan
Cambrai
St Quentin
La Fere
Laon
Soissons
Chantilly
Chateau Thierry
Epernay
Reims
Mont Blanc
PARIS
Noyan
Douai
Dracourt
Queant
Le Cateau
Maubeuge
Mons
BRUSSELS
Mezieres
Sedan
Verdun
St Mihiel
Metz

Scheldt
Somme
Meuse
Sambre
Aisne
Oise
Aisne
Marne
Seine
Moselle

Author's Note

In popular perception of the First World War – the public view – 1918 is a mystery. Everyone, it seems, has heard of the bloodletting on the Somme and perhaps Verdun in 1916, as well as the Third Ypres campaign or 'Passchendaele' in 1917. Most know vaguely about the Christmas Truce, which marked the end of universal hopes at the time of open warfare and marked the beginning of an unerring period of trench warfare, from the Channel Ports to the Swiss border on the Western Front, which was to last until 1918.

The opening gambit of the German offensives in 1918, popularly known as the *Kaiserschlacht*, or 'Emperor's Battle' is also fairly well known, but it was followed by a number of other attempts to force Allied capitulation and achieve a great German victory. But ultimately, all of the German offensives failed, despite some spectacular opening days, for a number of predictable reasons. They were disastrous short-comings in planning, strategy, intelligence and especially logistics. Similar failures would haunt the Third Reich between 1939 and 1945 and guarantee another humiliating nemesis for the German people.

Yet over the decades since the end of the First World War, few cataclysmic years in history have become more understood than 1918 and few historic events have been either misinterpreted or ignored as much as both the German and Allied ('Hundred Days') offensives respectively.

This book aims to redress the balance, or at least to reopen the debate about the reality and actual consequences of the military events of 1918 on the Western Front.

Ian Passingham,
Shepperton, December 2007

Acknowledgements

This Campaign Chronicle has a particular resonance for me, as it was the eve of the great offensives that began with the '*Kaiserschlacht*' that engendered an interest in the First World War for me as a youth thanks to the play 'Journey's End'. My desire to unearth the detail of the actual, rather than often mis-represented, events between March and the end of July 1918 has grown as I have learned much more over the years and also took the opportunity to work on German archives, as well as the more familiar British, Dominion and US primary and secondary sources.

Comparisons with both the style and content of German as opposed to the Allied regimental, divisional and official histories are endlessly engaging and often poignant. Equally, personal accounts have provided excellent testimony to the extraordinary courage and resolve of the BEF, French and, at times, US troops in stemming the German tide, as well as the bravery, sacrifice and ultimate disillusion of the German soldiers involved.

It has been an immense privilege to continue my association with the Imperial War Museum archive and library, the National Archives, Australian War Memorial, Bundesarchiv and the German Historical Institute. I have always received encouragement as well as impartial, professional and helpful advice during my digging and delving that is the lot of anyone trying to make some real sense of historic events. As always, the Imperial War Museum's Department of Printed Books, Documents and Mapping Department, as well as the Reading Room and Library have been outstandingly accommodating, as have the staff at the National Archives.

My enthusiasm for the subject of 'the Germans' in the First World War is constantly buoyed by the genuine interest and sheer stamina of

Acknowledgements

colleagues and friends from the Western Front Association (WFA), British Commission for Military History (BCMH), University of Birmingham Centre for First World War Studies and also Holts' Battlefield and History Tours. My thanks go to all who have kept me going, especially during the renowned 'third half' at meetings, conferences and on 'battlefield' tours.

The past decade has, at last, led to a greater desire for amateur and professional historians alike to learn and understand a great deal more of the German experience 1914–1918. I am delighted to note that Jack Sheldon has begun to take this interest to a higher level with two books on the German experience: of the Somme in 1916 and at Passchendaele. He is engaged also on a new range of 'Battlefield Europe' works on German units and formations that fought at such legendary places as Beaumont Hamel, the Schwaben Redoubt and Thiepval. Also, Chris Duffy has entered the arena with an excellent book on German views of the Allies during the Somme campaign. Many more publications of this type will follow and I welcome all such additions to the First World War historiography.

May I take this opportunity to acknowledge the extraordinary inspiration that so many sources have provided, not least of which was the brilliantly written and lovingly researched 'All Bloody Gentlemen' by the late Jill Knight, which so graphically describes the heroic fighting withdrawal of the 15th 'Londons' (Civil Service Rifles) in the darkest days of March 1918. Hugh Cleaver's detailed study on the pivotal events of 28th March was immensely helpful and I must make special mention also of the generous loan of some of the thousands of images of the First World War collected over the years by Giles Allen, a selection of which are reproduced here.

My thanks go to Pen & Sword for commissioning this Campaign Chronicle, especially to Rupert Harding. I am immensely grateful to the Series editor Chris Summerville for his excellent guidance and thank Pamela Covey for her due diligence in ensuring that the manuscript 'passed muster'.

Finally, it is an absolute fact that no such effort can be undertaken without the support and understanding of family and friends throughout the process of transforming an idea into the printed word. For the unstinting patience and encouraging words at even the most trying times, I salute you!

The German Offensives of 1918

While every effort has been made to acknowledge copyright holders of the references and illustrative material used in *'The German Offensives of 1918: The Last Desperate Gamble'*, should any copyright holders inadvertently have been omitted, I would urge them to contact the Publishers directly.

Background:
The Last Months
of 1917

On 6 November 1917 the Canadian Corps of the BEF[1] took the remnants of the Belgian village of Passchendaele. The enormous and bloody effort in achieving this aim – in what is officially known as the Third Ypres Campaign – was and remains a source of great debate, controversy and often emotive falsehoods inspired by such retrospective literature as Siegfried Sassoon's oft-quoted verse: 'They died in Hell – They called it Passchendaele.'

Nevertheless, the campaign hurt both sides and both sides marked it as a low-point in their respective fortunes. Crown Prince Rupprecht of Bavaria, whose Group of Armies included Fourth Army, which had borne the brunt of the fighting, was convinced that the experience was much worse for his men than those of the BEF. His Chief of Staff, General Hermann von Kuhl, called the 1917 Flanders Campaign 'The greatest martyrdom of the war'. The German soldier regarded this as an evil place, worse than their opponents, and one in which they believed that death or wounding was certain.

After tremendous courage and sacrifice on both sides, the BEF offensive officially ended on 10 November. The Allied and German casualties were approximately 250,000 on both sides, of which around one-third on each side were killed or posted as missing. The campaign had led to an advance of five miles, but the BEF had achieved few of its original major objectives and, despite the possession of the wasteland of Passchendaele, the northern sector of Passchendaele Ridge still lay in German hands.

For those who had fought in Flanders, little remained but to either consolidate gains or strengthen new defensive lines after the bloody loss of territory. Few imagined that another major attack, never mind an offensive, could be considered before the onset of winter. Battered and exhausted German regiments and a few divisions were sent south to Cambrai, which was known by a number of Germans as 'The Flanders Sanatorium', there to recuperate and regroup in a relatively quiet sector of the line. Not one man shed a tear for Flanders as he departed and few would dare to imagine they would return. Cambrai was, after all, a more peaceful place.

11 November 1917

By chance, the day after the Flanders Campaign closed proved to be a pivotal and strangely prophetic one in deciding the fate of the war itself. For on 11 November, one year to the day before the Armistice, the German High Command and Staff met at Mons. It marked the first of a series of crucial conferences that would determine the fate of Germany and guarantee final victory to the Allies ranged against her on the Western Front.

General Erich Ludendorff, the architect of what was to be Germany's final effort to prevail in the main theatre of war since 1914, considered the situation. First, it had become clear that the 1917 strategy of seeking a victory with unrestricted submarine warfare against British maritime supply lines had failed, especially as the Royal Navy's introduction of the convoy system had diminished the U-boat threat. Next, Russia was out of the war, so Ludendorff had the relative luxury of knowing that he could concentrate his resources in the West. The third external influence on the discussions was that of the USA.

With America's potential resources, not least of which was a fresh source of manpower, Ludendorff and his General Staff knew that the German Army could not afford to wait, or become embroiled in a protracted campaign. As the titular Quartermaster General of the German Armed Forces, he knew only too well that the Fatherland's resources were now finite, while, with America now included, Allied resources would be infinite.

Timing was crucial and Ludendorff believed that the spring of 1918 held the best opportunity for decisive action, as his Intelligence Staff convinced him that the British and French Armies were exhausted and divided as never before. So he and Field Marshal Paul von Hindenburg concluded that Germany now had but one chance to win the war. The main issue was whether to launch a major attack against the British or the French. Both reasoned that France was becoming increasingly dependent on her ally and that if the BEF was eradicated, France would be certain to sue for peace. With Russia out of the conflict, Ludendorff believed he would gather sufficient troops in the West to drive Field Marshal Sir Douglas Haig's BEF out of France and Flanders. With this in mind, he planned to destroy the British Army in France and Belgium while simultaneously cutting off the French to prevent their reinforcement of the BEF.

Strategy or Tactics?
Ludendorff's strategy, as it stood, was to be a fatal flaw. To him: 'Tactics had to be considered before purely strategical [sic] objects, which it is futile to pursue unless tactical success is possible. A strategic plan, which ignores the tactical factor, is foredoomed to failure ...' Wiser heads than his suggested that this view was generally contrary to accepted military thinking, but they were given short shrift. When battle commenced in March, Crown Prince Rupprecht was to ask for clarification on the German Army's strategic objective. Impatiently, Ludendorff retorted: 'I forbid myself to use the word "strategy". We chop a hole. The rest follows. We did it that way in Russia.' Unfortunately, the terrain and defences of the Western Front were quite different to those in the East. Furthermore, the quality of men and *matériel* available to both the British and French armies was in a different league to that of the Russians.

'We Must Beat the British'
Ludendorff's lofty assumption in November 1917 was that by February or March 1918 the German force on the Western Front would be irresistible. Based on this assumption, he laid down three conditions

General Erich Ludendorff (1865–1937)

Erich Ludendorff was born in Kruszwenia, near Poznan (modern Poland) in 1865. He was the son of a landowner, but came from a relatively modest background compared with many of his military peers. He was educated at the military school at Gross-Lichterfelde, Berlin and commissioned into an unglamorous infantry regiment, but quickly established himself as a professional, intelligent and ambitious young officer.

Ludendorff's determination and irrepressible energy marked him out from his contemporaries. General Helmuth von Moltke, the German Army Chief of Staff, who was to command the German Army in 1914, ensured that Ludendorff rose steadily through the ranks.

With the onset of war, Major General Ludendorff played a leading role in the capture of the seemingly impregnable Belgian fort at Liège during the German invasion of the West. For this, he was awarded the *Pour le Mérite*, Prussia's highest military honour. Later in August 1914 he became Chief of Staff to Field Marshal Paul von Hindenburg on the Eastern Front and assisted in forging the pivotal victories against the Russian army in 1914 and 1915.

In August 1916, as the battles of Verdun and the Somme raged on the Western Front, Ludendorff and Hindenburg became the joint heads of the whole German Army. The German casualties of almost a million men in these two battles were so large as to be almost insupportable. Ludendorff and Hindenburg swiftly decided that the only course open was to shorten the German line and give up some of the territory held since 1914. In March 1917, they withdrew their hard-pressed forces to the newly prepared defences of the Hindenburg Line, but not without controversy, as Ludendorff was the principal architect of the 'Scorched earth' policy that devastated much of the hitherto undamaged territory behind the then German lines.

Despite his undoubted moral courage, Ludendorff had become arrogant, inflexible and prone to panic when military operations did not go according to plan. After the failure of the German offensives in 1918, he became a broken man and following the further disaster of the Allied attack at Amiens on 8 August he knew that Germany's only practical course was to sue for peace. He was removed from command in October 1918 and replaced by Walter Groener.

Disillusioned by the circumstances of Germany's defeat and his own disgrace, Ludendorff gave his support to a former army corporal, believing that Adolf Hitler's extreme nationalism represented the only way for Germany to regain its honour. Ludendorff took part in Hitler's abortive *Putsch* in Munich in November 1923, and was tried for treason, but acquitted. Not until it was too late did he realize that Hitler was about to lead Germany once more into the abyss. Ludendorff died, fearful for his country's future, in 1937.

for a triumphant offensive. First, although the strength of the two sides was likely to be more or less equal across the Western Front, it was essential to concentrate his forces for the offensive and achieve a breakthrough with one critical onslaught. Despite advice to the contrary, he was adamant that an alternative offensive, even as a diversion, was out of the question as it was impossible on any reasonable scale. The second condition was that the main blow must fall against the British 'at the earliest possible moment'. Finally, he stated simply that: 'We must beat the British.'

Ludendorff's Principal Operations Adviser Counsels Caution

Opposing this view, *Oberstleutnant* Georg Wetzell, the German Army's chief of operational planning, warned him that 'any prospect of success in the West depends upon other principles than those which hold good for the East or against Italy' and subsequently produced a more practical plan for an attack in the West.

Wetzell warned Ludendorff that the successful modus operandi of military operations against the Russian Army in particular were not likely to guarantee victory against the French and British, and that a breakthrough was almost impossible to envisage in a single assault on either the French or British sectors. This would facilitate the Allied defence, for they could bring their resources to bear to foil the German thrust.

Wetzell recommended a strategy that would cause maximum disruption to the British or French response: attacks in two or three sectors in order to unhinge any enemy defensive strategy and deceive him into the premature use of any strategic reserve. In the first phase, the British reserves would be drawn to the St Quentin sector, where the offensive would be carried only as far as a line from Bapaume to La Fère, north to south. The second phase would mask the movement of the 'great battering train' of heavy guns, mortars and aircraft of the High Command's strategic reserve, alongside a massive concentration of infantry divisions, which would smash through the British defences on the Flanders front. Then the decisive phase would be an overwhelming onslaught through Flanders and the seizure of the critical town of Hazebrouck, thus cutting the bulk of the BEF off from its reinforcement and supply lines via the Channel ports.

Ludendorff's Choice is to Throw Caution to the Wind

Erich Ludendorff would not be dissuaded. From the outset, he seemed certain that one massive offensive across the Somme sector would offer the best opportunity for a swift victory. However, a firm decision on this option and other main contenders, which included an assault across Flanders and a breakthrough against the well-defended Scarpe/Arras sector, would have to wait until the latter part of January 1918. In any option, success would depend entirely on surprise, overwhelming strength in the chosen sector and an immediate paralysis of the British defensive spirit, overwhelmed by the German maelstrom as they stormed the BEF positions.

All the senior German commanders and Staff Officers knew that if the initial offensive failed to achieve a decisive breakthrough, the opportunity for victory would fade rapidly and could not be matched on quite the same scale again. Army group and army commanders already had their doubts and most agreed that the choice of attacking the BEF rather than the French in this 'decisive' offensive was a high-risk strategy, based on a gambler's all-or-nothing stake.

It was to be Ludendorff's last desperate gamble.

20 November 1917: Cambrai – The British 'Mailed Fist' leaves Ludendorff Punch-Drunk

Just over one week later, the German High Command and the soldiers of General von der Marwitz's Second Army, defending the Cambrai sector, were themselves surprised and brought to the brink of humiliation by a bold British attack that was to prove an ominous

Background: The Last Months of 1917

sign of what was to come in 1918. At 0610 hours on 20 November, the silence of a misty morning was broken by the clanking sound of tanks and the drone of British aircraft flying low over the German lines. At 0620 hours, the tanks and assaulting infantry crossed the 'Start Line' and appeared, closing in on the German front line. German resistance was immediately broken by the thunder of a massive, sudden bombardment by over 1,000 guns, which raked the German defensive lines, artillery batteries and HQ positions in the Rear Zones.

A total of 378 Mark IV tanks, supported by six infantry assault divisions on a 6-mile front burst into the German Defensive Zone of Battlegroup (Gruppe) Caudry. German battalion and company commanders and their men were stunned by the sheer scale of the British armoured/infantry assault and the sudden, devastating 'predicted' artillery fire. At first, though some resourceful and fearless German resistance was put up, most of the survivors in the defensive Outpost Zone either surrendered or fled. Many of the retreating men were then killed by their own defensive artillery or mortar fire as they ran back to their second-line trenches. One Corporal (*Obergefreiter*) later recorded that:

> There had not been any hint whatever of any preparation of an attack [...] nothing extraordinary on a seemingly thin, quiet front [...] [Then] only after the attack started did we realize what was going to happen. The British forces, strengthened by hundreds of tanks, could move freely and overthrew our thin defences.

In an almost futile gesture, some German artillery units responded with weak counter-battery fire, but the British advance was so swift that most of the German shells fell behind the tanks and assaulting infantry.

When the main defences of the Hindenburg Line in this sector were reached by the leading waves of British tanks and infantry, German resistance stiffened and some attacking infantry battalions were held up by machine-gun, trench mortar and rifle fire. But the massed tanks pushed on, crushing the thick belts of barbed wire and a number of

The German Offensives of 1918

German machine-gun crews in their wake. Ludendorff underlined the extent of the German surprise when he noted that:

> In the West the crisis caused by the Battle of Flanders, the Battle of the Laffaux salient [in the French sector] and their after effects, passed away. We were expecting a continuation of the attacks in Flanders and on the French front, when on the 20th of November we were surprised by a fresh blow at Cambrai.

By the afternoon of 20 November, Ludendorff and Rupprecht had agreed that the desperate situation must be restored by a planned counterstroke. But that would take time and reinforcements that were not available to punch their way out of the corner that Gruppe Caudry was caught in. The crisis grew as each hour passed. The German 54th Division and its artillery lost most of its fighting strength and its defences were almost non-existent by the end of the day. A total of 5,785 officers and men were killed or missing and a further 5,000 men wounded or taken as prisoners. The 84th Regiment had its regimental commander and the COs of all three battalions killed and its strength reduced to around 30 per cent of its original force. The other front-line divisions suffered almost as badly as the 54th, although it had borne the brunt of the British attacks.

The situation became so grim that serious plans were made for a general withdrawal and the demolition of the canal bridges in front of Cambrai. The Camp Commandant of 54th Divisional HQ was sent with an *ad hoc* platoon of three officers and thirty men to defend the canal crossings at Marcoing and Masnières, and for several hours in the afternoon of the first day there was a totally undefended one-mile gap in the Masnières-Beaurevoir defence line between Masnières and Crèvecoeur.

By pure chance, the British failed to identify this yawning gap before it was plugged and the extraordinary advance began to lose some of its steam as the day drew to a close. Twentieth November was nevertheless considered to be a British triumph and church bells rang throughout the country to celebrate a great victory. Sadly, the celebrations were a little premature ...

Background: The Last Months of 1917

Trust in God and von der Marwitz

By midnight on that same day, Gruppe Caudry was strengthened by the 107th Division and regiments pulled from both Gruppe Arras to the Cambrai sector's north and Gruppe St Quentin to the south. Three more divisions (119th of Fourth Army, 30th of Seventh Army and 214th of Sixth Army) were rushed towards the Cambrai. All arrived within forty-eight hours.

From the German point of view, the possibility of utter disaster had been averted – just. Regardless of this, the situation remained perilous for some days. Desperate messages to divisional and regimental HQs came in thick and fast from the sorely pressed front-line units by telephone, runner, pigeon or messenger dogs.

As the days passed after 20 November, the German defences were reinforced and resistance hardened as the British 'punch' lost its hitting power. Crown Prince Rupprecht and his army commander von der Marwitz lost no time in planning a stunning counterblow as the day-to-day fighting continued in the guts of the Cambrai defence.

Counter-Attack

As the remnants of Gruppe Caudry's front-line divisions and their reinforcements slugged it out against the remaining British tanks and infantry assaults, a new command, Gruppe Bussigny (based on XXIII Korps), was formed and commanded by General von Kathen, a tough and experienced senior officer. On 24 November preliminary orders were issued by Rupprecht's Chief of Staff, General Hermann von Kuhl that a counter-offensive was to be launched 'at an early date'. The Bussigny, Caudry and Arras Battlegroups were all tasked for the offensive.

Rupprecht discussed the proposed plan with Ludendorff and von der Marwitz at HQ Second Army in Le Cateau and then issued orders for the counter-offensive to Second Army on the evening of the 27th. The attack was to be launched on 30 November. Gruppe Bussigny, supported by Gruppe Caudry, would attack from the south-east into the British flank and rear and recapture Flesquières and Havrincourt. Gruppe Arras was then to launch a heavy attack from the Bourlon Wood area towards the south.

9

The German Offensives of 1918

30 November 1917: German Innovation on a Grander Scale – Stormtroops Arise!

The outline plan of attack for the German counter-offensive at Cambrai was straightforward enough. But novel tactics were used on a grander scale than previously attempted to infiltrate and overwhelm the hastily prepared British defences. A short but intensive artillery bombardment, using both gas and high explosive shells, was to be followed by an infantry assault in which the lightly equipped but heavily armed leading waves were ordered to bypass villages and strongpoints, infiltrate the British positions and then neutralize or destroy HQs and British artillery batteries.

The spearhead of the attack was to be led by troops with bags full of grenades and armed with light machine guns, light mortars and flame-throwers. The assaults were to be accompanied by 77mm field artillery batteries moving forward as rapidly as possible to provide anti-tank fire and close support for the attacking infantry.

The vital ingredient for the success of these tactics would be the same as that for the British on 20 November: surprise.

Until the evening of 29 November, General von der Marwitz and Rupprecht doubted that surprise could possibly be achieved. Both were convinced that the British must have been aware of increased German movements in the last few days and expected British trench raids and strong hostile air activity, but they failed to materialize. The night of 29/30 November was unusually quiet and the final German infantry deployment into jumping off positions was made without interference.

Zero Hour: A German Riposte

At 0600 hours on 30 November, the German guns opened up on the British 55th Division and the bombardment gradually spread across the southern sector of the Cambrai front. Within half an hour it reached a crescendo of withering gas, high explosive and mortar fire, which caused havoc in many forward defences and cut most of the communications to the rear of the British positions.

Zero Hour was at precisely 0700 hours. At that moment, German infantry swarmed across no-man's-land under cover of a devastating artillery barrage, a thick mist and scant daylight. At daybreak, German

Background: The Last Months of 1917

aircraft filled the sky and sought their revenge for the humiliation of being caught on the ground on 20 November, bombing rear positions and strafing British troops wherever possible. It was to be a day of mayhem across the Cambrai front, as the German assaults were pressed home against amazingly stiff British resistance, despite the initial shock of the German assault.

Leutnant Ernst Jünger of 73rd Hanoverian Fusilier Regiment went into the initial assault and reflected the German and British experiences of that day:

> At 7 [a.m.] sharp we advanced in single file [and found] Dragon Alley unoccupied [...] We then entered the trench on the right. It was full of arms and equipment and English dead. It was the Siegfried Line [Hindenburg Line] [...] Going further we met with resolute resistance [...] and we were driven back [...] Then we took part in another assault [...] The English resisted valiantly. Every traverse was contested. Mills bombs and stick grenades crossed and recrossed. Behind each we found dead or still quivering bodies. We killed each other out of sight ...

In the afternoon, attacking German troops were subjected to determined counter-attacks and heavy artillery fire, but by the evening the British had been severely mauled.

Losses were heavy on both sides, with Jünger among the badly wounded, and the German infiltration methods often led to a loss of control, as troops assigned to this specialist role had not received sufficient training. Also, Ludendorff later suggested that:

> The success was all the more remarkable because it was in the main achieved by half-tired troops who had not been specially trained for attack.

At the other end of the scale, *Obergefreiter* Franz Benöhr, who had recovered from the shock of the first day of the British onslaught, noted later that:

> [Many of the tanks] moved so quickly at the beginning that they got lost and were then destroyed by our guns [...] Having arrived

on the outskirts of Cambrai they had to stop for a day or two for reorganization, replenishment and the like. Then it was too late for them to move on: Strong German reinforcements arrived and stopped the British attack.

The German Counter-Offensive Runs out of Steam

The battle raged on for a further four days, although much of the most intensive fighting took place on the first two. By 5 December both sides were completely exhausted. The battle ended virtually in the original British front line in the early hours of 20 November.

Between 20 November and 5 December 1917, Crown Prince Rupprecht was forced to use twenty infantry divisions against the British Third Army's fifteen infantry and four cavalry divisions, in addition to the 386 Mark IV tanks involved on Day One of the offensive.

The part played by the RFC in the British attacks, and the German Air Arm during the German counter-offensive, was of immense value to the ground troops they supported, but losses were high on both sides.

Overall, the German Second Army lost around 45,000 killed, missing, wounded and prisoners and the British just over 44,000 men at Cambrai. As usual in war, statistics conceal the bitter truth and tragedy of the casualties they represent.

Reflections

Cambrai was a grim end to a gruesome year. Most of those who had survived it on the Western front, regardless of their uniform, saw nothing more than a dark horizon looming as a portent for 1918.

Regimental records from both sides of the wire reflect the melancholy in considering the prospects for the coming year, as well as the frustration of once more failing to produce a decisive result by the end of 1917. For the BEF, despite the brilliant start and the heavy punishment inflicted on the Germans, 'Cambrai' had provoked real concern for the future.

A tremendous opening day, with innovations such as the predicted and short bombardment and massed use of tanks and all-arms to catch the German defenders off guard, was countered by the strength

Background: The Last Months of 1917

and vigour of the German counterstroke. Furthermore, the German reserves thrown in came from the now redundant Eastern Front, some of the first of an increasing number of reinforcements that would move from Russia to the Western Front by spring 1918. Both Russia and Romania had finally capitulated in the first few days of December, enabling Germany to accelerate the transfer of infantry and artillery divisions to the West. Thirty-three infantry divisions within a number of corps would augment those already in France and Belgium by 1 January 1918.

But this bonus for the German High Command hardly reflected the 'poor bloody infantry' that would be obliged to do the fighting and dying in 1918 for the 'promise of victory'. At regimental level, German units were heartened by the relative success of the Cambrai counterstroke and victory in Russia, although many were bitter and resented their predicament. They saw little prospect of a 'Triumph in the West'. German morale was generally low, despite the propaganda at the time, Ludendorff's and von Hindenburg's memoirs and the often ill-informed historical analysis of more recent years. The unrest, poverty and hunger back home in Germany affected the ordinary German soldier, which was hardly boosted by the fact that troops were not well fed at the front. It was a bad time for most German troops by the final months of 1917. Combat fatigue was not the only thing that gnawed away at their very fibre. Their demeanour was stoic, but their opinion of those at home who profited from their suffering was scathing:

> We [ordinary German soldiers] are emaciated and starved. Our food is bad and mixed up with so much substitute (ersatz) stuff that it makes us ill. The factory owners in Germany have grown wealthy [but here] dysentery dissolves our bowels [...]

The BEF Takes Stock

On the British side, most felt that they had come through the year with tantalizing glimpses of the ultimate superiority of the Allied War Machine over that of Germany's. However, the winter was to offer little encouragement and one marked feature noted by many British

Field Marshal Paul (Ludwig Hans Anton) von Beneckendorff und von Hindenburg (1847–1934)

Paul von Hindenburg was born in 1847 into a family of the traditional Prussian military aristocracy. A handsome and determined individual as a boy, he became a military cadet, excelled in his peer group and was commissioned at the age of eighteen into the élite Prussian Foot Guards.

He fought with distinction in both the Austro-Prussian and Franco-Prussian wars, and was decorated for bravery in 1870. Following the Franco-Prussian war, he continued to follow a military career, and rose steadily through the ranks. Count Alfred von Schlieffen, the mastermind behind German strategy in 1914, was due to retire in 1904, and Hindenburg, now a full General himself, was tipped to replace him. However, during the final exercise of the annual military manoeuvres in 1905, he had the misfortune to defeat the Kaiser. Realizing that this was not good for his career, Hindenburg resigned. He later wrote: 'My military career had carried me much further than I had dared hope. There was no prospect of war at the time [...] so I applied to retire.'

Although still an active patron of the military, including the Franco-Prussian War Veterans' Association, Hindenburg was frustrated by his inactivity in retirement. But he hardly expected to be recalled for active service when war erupted in August 1914. By the third week in August, General von Moltke, the German Army commander, realized that things were not going well against Russia. He appointed General Erich Ludendorff as the new Chief of Staff in East Prussia, with Hindenburg as the commander of the German Eighth Army. Under this new team, with the brilliant Staff Officer Colonel Max Hoffmann providing the plan, the German Eighth Army trounced two Russian armies at Tannenberg (August 1914) and Hindenburg was given the accolade 'Hero of Tannenberg'. The magnitude of the Russian defeat so early in the war caused psychological damage from which her army never fully recovered.

Von Hindenburg was promoted to Field Marshal and became a national icon. Tannenberg also forged the partnership between Hindenburg and Ludendorff, which would oversee Germany's military strategy for the last two years of the First World War. But from early 1917, Hindenburg's influence was diminished as Ludendorff took hold of the

Background: The Last Months of 1917

reins of power. The situation continued until the last month of the war. After Armistice and Versailles, Hindenburg's credibility remained so high amongst the ordinary German people that he became President of the Weimar Republic.

Later, he attempted to limit the burgeoning power of Adolf Hitler, whom he disliked intensely, but was forced to make Chancellor in January 1933. Hindenburg died, aged eighty-seven, in August 1934. He was buried at a newly erected shrine near Tannenberg, the scene of his greatest triumph, with full ceremony. It was an ironic twist of fate that Hitler was the architect of Hindenburg's solemn and respectful funeral ceremony. With Hindenburg's death, Hitler gained absolute power and set Germany on a course that was to prove even more disastrous than of 1914 to 1918.

battalions in the line was the increased aggressiveness of the Germans, as trench raids were carried out in earnest.

Most importantly, there was a noticeably sluggish reinforcement rate into battered battalions, or within the more routine roulement of new troops drafted after training into infantry battalions, artillery batteries, RE Companies and across the BEF ORBAT.[2] At the time, few of the front-line units were aware that this was not as a result of lack of manpower, but rather decisions being made in London on holding back reinforcements throughout the winter and forthcoming spring.

Haig was to request a total of 334,000 reinforcements between December 1917 and March 1918 and receive a mere 174,000. British PM Lloyd George saw the limiting of reinforcements sent to France and Belgium as one method of curtailing Haig's use of his men in costly offensives, although it was actually CIGS 'Wully' Robertson and the War Office that kept the general reserve back in the UK. This feeling, together with Haig's own estimate in a communiqué to Robertson that he could resist a major German attack against the British sector on the Western Front for at least eighteen days, led to the policy of 'holding back'.

However, one organizational effect of the policy was the reduction in strength of most of the BEF's infantry divisions from twelve to

15

The German Offensives of 1918

Pioneer Battalions

A pioneer battalion was added to the establishment between late 1915 and mid-1916 (although some divisions serving in Mesopotamia used various units of the Indian Army for similar purposes). A Divisional Employment Company of the Labour Corps was added too, in 1917. By 1918, the establishment was usually 4 officers and 313 other ranks, although numbers fluctuated depending on the job in hand and the availability of lines of communication, corps or army troops. All too often, though, the infantry had to be used for manual labour tasks.

Source: Chris Baker, *The Long, Long Trail* website.

---

nine battalions throughout February and early March 1918. Of the British units in France and Belgium, 115 were disbanded, thirty-eight amalgamated to produce nineteen 'composite' battalions and a further seven were converted from infantry, primarily to pioneer battalions. On the other hand, this reorganization did not affect the Dominion and US units. The New Zealand Division, five Australian and four Canadian divisions, which were to form the ANZAC and Canadian Corps, retained twelve battalions.

When they were in force on the Western Front, US divisions would be around twice the size of British and French divisions, but by December 1917 there were little more than 130,000 American troops in place and US commander General 'Black Jack' Pershing was well aware that months of further reinforcement and training lay ahead before the American Expeditionary Force, or AEF, was ready to take its place in the Allied line in a truly meaningful way.

Dead Reckoning: The Cost of 1917

By the end of 1917 Germany had lost at least 1,297,750 killed or missing, presumed dead. Surely, with Russia now out of the war, prospects for 1918 could only be better? It was by no means certain, despite the renewed confidence amongst the German High Command.

From a broader perspective, 1917 has been depicted as one of disappointment and bloody sacrifice on the Allied side, but with little, or any, general comment on the state of the opposition – i.e. Germany –

Background: The Last Months of 1917

over the same 365-day period. One cannot dismiss or deny the fact that it was a bad year from the Allied angle in many ways, as it often promised so much, but achieved so little on the face of it. The BEF had taken the main strain on the Western Front after the depressing failure of the much-lauded French-inspired Nivelle offensive in April/May 1917, which had led to General Robert Nivelle's removal as French C-in-C within six months of his appointment, and the mutinies that had crippled French fighting spirit and capability for months afterwards.

Meanwhile, the Allied successes at Arras/Vimy Ridge in April, Messines in June and the opening phase of Cambrai in November 1917 had each resulted in failure to achieve wider objectives. Also, the Allied Intelligence Staff had not assessed the extraordinary ability of the German Army to recover and hit back when given the opportunity to do so.

The BEF, Allied Commitments and Political/Military Differences

By December 1917 it was evident to the Allied political and military leaders that they would have to anticipate a major German effort to force a decision on the Western Front. It was here that the war was to be won or lost – as it had been since August 1914. Regardless of previous failed offensives on the Western Front, it was clear that Germany would have no choice but to launch an offensive. No war was ever won with a purely defensive strategy and in this case, American manpower and resources would tip the balance in favour of the Allies if Germany's leaders did not switch to an offensive strategy in the early part of 1918.

Unlike the remainder of the belligerent powers in the First World War, the BEF never came close to rebellion or mutiny. Etaples, which is so often cited as an example of how close 'we' came to undermining British military authority, was and remains a convenient 'red herring' for those who wish to exploit it as an example of the potential disintegration of the BEF out of context.

Equally true, the BEF casualty bills resulting from Arras, Third Ypres/Passchendaele and Cambrai added critical fuel to the fire of CIGS 'Wully' Robertson and British PM David Lloyd George's criticism of Field Marshal Sir Douglas Haig.

17

The German Offensives of 1918

Worse for the 'field' commanders on the Western Front, General Sir Edmund 'Bull' Allenby's success in taking Jerusalem in December 1917 gave hope to British and French advocates of an 'Eastern solution' as the panacea for final victory. Regardless of the faults that have been heaped on Haig since his death, he never doubted where his opponents, von Falkenhayn and then Hindenburg and Ludendorff, knew that the war would be decided, namely the Western Front. Haig's intuition was unequivocal and correct.

As a result of all of these considerations, Lloyd George was reluctant to crack open a political and royal hornet's nest by sacking Haig, who had a very close and trusted liaison with King George V. However, he was looking for ways to reduce the power and influence of both Haig and CIGS Robertson and was actively considering assigning both to appointments that were prestigious but without influence. Lloyd George was surprised (and perhaps a little shocked) to discover that Haig and his GHQ Staff were generally well regarded and trusted by formation and unit level commanders and the men who served under them.

Regardless of Haig's close liaison with the Royal family, he was loyal to his Staff, his army commanders and the BEF troops that he had the privilege to orchestrate. Lloyd George's vitriol against some British commanders, and Haig in particular, would not be apparent until later, following the publication of memoirs in which, having had time to reconsider the reality of events, he added some self-serving 'spin'. So the BEF Command structure remained virtually intact into early 1918.

The French Perspective

From the French perspective, Marshal Henri Philippe Pétain had proved well suited to the task of gradually reinvigorating the Poilus'[3] belief in their fighting ability and reviving morale after the dreadful experience of Verdun, the Somme campaigns in 1916, and the disastrous Nivelle offensive in April/May 1917. The French Army proved its mettle in two successful limited offensives at Verdun in August and the Chemin des Dames in October 1917, fine achievements often ignored when reviewing the situation in the latter months of 1917. However, despite this affirmation of a renewed confidence, the French Army would still

Background: The Last Months of 1917

have to be tested as a major attacking force once more, and it would be months before such an opportunity would present itself again.

Like the BEF, the bottom of the French manpower barrel was thinly covered and at least three divisions were disbanded and a further six sent to augment Allied forces in Italy. At the end of December 1917, France had a total of 100 infantry divisions on the Western Front and each one was down to no more than 6,000 infantry of a total establishment of some 15,000 personnel per division.

Politically, France had been in turmoil for much of 1917. Winston Churchill had summed up the situation by proclaiming that the French Republic hung for years by a thread. Georges Clemenceau, the 'Tiger' by reputation for his ruthlessness and iron will, was swept back to power in November. In strident mood, he appeared before the French Chamber of Deputies on the 20th of that month – the same day as the BEF was making terrific headway on day one of the Cambrai offensive – to ask for the Chamber's confidence in his 'way forward'. His presentation was a *tour de force*. In it he maintained:

We have accepted the government in order to conduct the war with redoubled energy [...] There will be no consideration of persons or partisan passions; no more pacifist campaigns, no treachery [...] only war. Nothing but war! [...] The country shall know that it is being defended.

Churchill was in attendance and later wrote that the 76-year-old ball of energetic fire was:

Like a wild animal pacing to and fro growling and glaring [...] France had resolved to unbar the cage and let the tiger loose upon all foes [...] Language, elegance and arguments were not needed [here]. With snarls and growls, the ferocious, aged, dauntless beast of prey went into action.

No one within the Chamber of Deputies on that day – and within the French population from the following day – was under any illusion or had any uncertainty who was in charge from now on. For the time being, French democracy took a back seat and a tacit understanding existed that Clemenceau was a 'benign' dictator, but at least with the understanding that when he had served his purpose he would happily stand down, or be dismissed by popular vote.

The Allied experience of 1917 did at least encourage a positive step towards a more coherent coordination of Allied strategy. In the same month of November the Allied Supreme War Council was convened at Versailles.

Russian Collapse

On 7 November 1917, the Bolshevik revolution was pronounced when Lenin's cohorts wrested what little power remained from Romanov hands and immediately took steps to accommodate Ludendorff and Hindenburg's desire for victory in the East by force of arms. All Russian military resistance officially ended on 28 November and armistice terms were agreed with Germany and Austria-Hungary by 15 December. Full peace negotiations were initiated at Brest-Litovsk on 20 December and they would take over two difficult months to be concluded and, ultimately, to the satisfaction of few on either side. Worst of all, the German victory over Russia would lead to a considerably greater military commitment than anticipated, divert Ludendorff's attention in the first two and a half months of 1918, and have critical consequences once the German offensives were launched in the West.

The United States and the German Fear Factor

As 1917 drew to a close, German relief and celebration of Russia's apparent nemesis was tempered strongly by the question of the 'new enemy'. Actually, the greatest harm the United States was to inflict on Germany was the deeply damaging psychological blow already thrown on 6 April 1917. The mere fact that America had entered the war formally on that day was enough to upset the bloody but delicate equilibrium that existed between the Allies and the Central Powers. The pressure of the growing number of American troops in France meant that the German Army must strike quickly. The United States had been contributing to the Allied military-industrial output for much of the war, and since April 1917, the manpower was available

Background: The Last Months of 1917

to make good the French and British losses. Ludendorff knew that the American troops would be fit, well-nourished and keen as mustard to 'get at the Boche'.

However, the promised American troops had so far failed to materialize in great numbers: only four US divisions were deployed in France by the end of 1917, and only one was 'in the line'. In addition, the US commander, General John Joseph 'Black Jack' Pershing, was under strict orders from Washington not to use his men piecemeal to reinforce the stretched British and French formations, but to keep his battalions and divisions together as a distinct entity under the title of the American Expeditionary Force, or AEF.

Ludendorff saw this as a golden opportunity to exploit in early spring 1918. But he knew that the German offensive in the West would have to win a swift victory or disaster would surely follow with the irresistible American build-up.

Ludendorff had some foundation for his optimism, for as the New Year beckoned, he took heart from the German stand on the Western Front and victory in the East, as well as the success of more widely used artillery and stormtroops tactics at Riga, Caporetto and Cambrai, and the transfer of new blood to bolster his depleted formations in the West from Russia.

But Ludendorff, Hindenburg and the Kaiser had much cause for anxiety too. The effects of the Allied Naval Blockade, so often ignored in reviews or analyses of the war in general and 1918 in particular, were now manifest in a significant shortage of horses, fodder, petrol, oil, rubber, iron and steel. These deficiencies would have a profound effect on the mobility of the German Army in 1918 and thus the High Command's ability to sustain the offensive now in its planning stage. Mobility was reliant on horse-drawn wagons, motor transport and an effective narrow-gauge railway system to resupply armies at the front with the necessary *matériel* – especially manpower and artillery ammunition.

Therefore, Germany would be short of so many essential parts of its war machine before the first shot was fired in 1918. Ludendorff, as the German Quartermaster General, must have realized the scale of the problem when he was informed that German infantry had faltered in their pursuit of a retreating British unit at Cambrai when the troops

The German Offensives of 1918

Stormtroops

The German troops began their final training for the March 1918 offensive in the West. They were certain that the deadlock would soon be over. One man wrote: 'Every German soldier on the Western Front felt that the decision of war and peace was at hand.'

The preparations for the offensive had been intense. Training centres were established in each army area. All infantry divisions, including those being transferred from the East to the Western Front, were given special instruction in infiltration techniques.

Units already in the line were combed for the youngest, fittest and most battle-hardened men. These would become the backbone of the special stormtroop detachments. Surprise and speed were the stormtroops' principal tactics.

Many stormtroops were issued with the 9mm MP18 Bergmann submachine-gun, a novel weapon that was designed for close-quarter battle (CQB) and most of the company and platoon officers carried revolvers. However, the vast majority of the stormtroopers still carried the 7.92mm Gewehr common to the German Army. The ubiquitous stick-grenade, or 'potato-masher' as it was known by the British soldiers, was one of the assault units' main weapons, held in special shoulder-slung pouches. This was characteristic of the *Eingreif*, or counter-attack troops used in defensive tactics prior to the great offensive.

Specially trained stormtroop squads also used flame-throwers, machine guns and trench mortars. German artillerymen were trained to shoot accurate artillery bombardments using maps rather than actual gunfire to register the guns on their targets, a method that had been used with such effect by the British prior to the opening phase of the Battle of Cambrai in November 1917.

found and looted a captured BEF supply depot. It was an isolated incident, but it made Ludendorff and his Staff realise that German resources could not hope to match those of the Allies if the planned spring offensive failed to deliver a rapid victory.

Worse, the battles of 1917 actually offered a great deal of encouragement to the Allies and the BEF in particular. Among its achievements had been the successful storming of Vimy Ridge in April, and that of Messines in June, as well as General Sir Herbert Plumer's meticulous set-piece assaults in the drier, warmer, weather of September and the

Background: The Last Months of 1917

first days of October during the Third Ypres campaign. Novel artillery methods and the massed tank assault at Cambrai succeeded in penetrating the much-vaunted 'impregnable' defences of the Hindenburg Line in November. Above all, despite the disappointment of the year, the BEF's morale was still intact and the Allies had, at least, the prospect of an endless stream of manpower and resources to draw upon in 1918: that of the USA.

Germany had no such luxury.

One thing was for certain: a German triumph had to be assured within weeks of the opening of the great offensive 'or the Fatherland's military and political nemesis would be assured'.

Campaign Chronicle

———— ◦ ⦁ ◦ ————

On 1 January 1918 the Kaiser and his closest advisers were in Berlin. Many people in the capital and across the Fatherland awoke that morning with a depressing feeling that the next twelve months would represent nothing more than another 365 days of sacrifice at home and at the front.

Not surprisingly, the view from the Kaiser's Court was different. One of the Kaiser's closest advisers, Admiral Georg von Müller noted: 'New Year's Day, which throughout Germany and the whole of the world has been greeted as the year of peace, began with a cold and dreary day.'

But with stoic faith, the majority of German citizens prayed that this would be a decisive year; just as they had in July and August 1914 and the New Year's Days of 1915, 1916 and 1917. What they did know was that every passing day had to be a day closer to the end of the war, but no one knew how many days, weeks or months that would take, or how long it would take for the suffering to end on the Home Front even after victory or defeat.

Germany had suffered badly in 1917 and the people had managed to prevail, but only just. Regardless of the relief that the war against Russia was over, few Germans had cause for any celebration. The war continued everywhere else and millions of Germans on the Home Front were on the brink of starvation and many had succumbed to

January 1918: Germany – A Troubled Land

disease brought on by malnourishment and poor medical facilities. Throughout 1917, the grim reality of life in Germany haunted families at home and the loved ones who were fighting at the front.

It had all gone horribly wrong and, with the exception of the profiteers and a healthy black market, the ordinary German people existed in a surreal, ersatz[4] life where everyone seemed to be devoured with a desperate anxiety about the dearth of food resources for the winter. Coffee and tea were almost impossible to obtain and that which was sold was made of 'all sorts of berries and leaves' as a surrogate. Butter, meat and bread were equally scarce for ordinary folk – or still bountiful for the few who could afford black market prices. Terrible shortages, ill-health and dark thoughts about the millions of German sons who were already dead or scarred for life left Germany in a very black public mood. It was a sorry, pitiful and precarious platform from which the German military dictatorship was planning to launch a final massive bid for victory.

Anyone within the upper echelons of German society in Berlin was aware that major decisions were being discussed and made in this early week or two of the New Year and speculation mounted as to why there was: '[A] never-ending crisis in Government affairs going on. Hindenburg and Ludendorff, as well as the Crown Prince, are in Berlin and important conferences are always taking place.'

So wrote Evelyn Blücher at that time and her observations were accurate enough. German political, military and imperial egos were about to compete for the high ground in an inevitable clash of the titans.

January 1918: Germany – A Troubled Land

The popular perception of Germany at the beginning of 1918 tends to be one of a resurgent nation, boosted by her victory in the East and confident of an even greater triumph on the Western Front before the summer of that year. Indeed, there were some who would have considered August as a perfect solution, as it would have provided a neat reminder that Germany would have succeeded after exactly four years of 'victorious struggle'. At least the war would be over by Christmas ... again.

25

The German Offensives of 1918

In fact, this perception could not be further from the truth. In January 1918, public loyalty and respect towards the Kaiser were diminishing rapidly. Unrest was rife across Germany as conditions continued to deteriorate; politicians and the military leadership were openly criticized and there was little enthusiasm for yet more bloody sacrifice of fathers, brothers, sons and friends at the front. The days of the Hohenzollern Dynasty were surely numbered, as the Kaiser had lost any vestige of real authority once the 'Duumvirate' of Hindenburg and especially Ludendorff was installed at the head of the German Military Machine.

Erich Ludendorff took stock of the situation as the New Year dawned and later noted:

> Owing to the breakdown of Russia the military situation was more favourable to us at New Year, 1918, than could have ever been expected. As in 1914 and 1915, we could think of deciding the war by an attack on land. Numerically, we had never been so strong in comparison with our enemies [...] In the late autumn of 1917, GHQ was confronted by the decisive question: Should it utilize the favourable conditions of the spring to strike a great blow in the West, or should it deliberately restrict itself to the defensive [...]? In Germany the national spirit appeared to be better than with our Allies; nevertheless, it had sunk very low and feeling had become worse. I must admit [that at the time] I formed too favourable an estimate of our remaining energy [...] [As the front] The Army had come victoriously through 1917; but it had become apparent that holding the Western Front purely by a defensive could no longer be counted on [...] The troops had borne the continuous defensive with extreme difficulty [...] [and] against the weight of the enemy's material the troops no longer displayed their old stubbornness; they thought with horror of fresh defensive battles and longed for the war of movement [...] The interests of the Army were best served by the offensive [...] This feeling was shared by everybody. In the West the Army pined for the offensive, and after Russia's collapse expected it with the most intense relief. Such was the feeling of the troops about attack and defence.

21 January: Decision Time

Perhaps it was true that many German military leaders and their troops were ' "pining" for an offensive' in the West. After all, it was Ludendorff who acknowledged that: 'The offensive is the most effective means of making war; it alone is decisive.' But, for most soldiers either in the West already the prospect of offensive action was as depressing as holding the line against the enemy.

Ludendorff and Hindenburg would soon roll out the 1918 version of the ritual New Year promise of victory, but few would believe it unless it was tied to a firmer undertaking to win the war on the Home Front too. The German people steeled themselves for another massive military effort and another year of civilian deprivation, ill-health, and yet more belt-tightening to see them through to an inevitable end – glorious or otherwise. To many it was undoubtedly the most dangerous and uncertain adventure of the whole war. On behalf of the Fatherland and in the name of the Kaiser, Ludendorff was about to throw down the gauntlet to fate and against an enemy who, if not crushed quickly, would destroy Germany.

21 January: Decision Time

On 21 January, two months before the 'main event', Erich Ludendorff finally made his choice of the original three options for the great offensive to come. The strongest candidates that had emerged from the planning process in the winter were: Operation George – the mass attack through Flanders; Operation Mars, which would take the Arras/Vimy area head-on; and, finally, Operation Michael – the thrust through the battle-scarred Somme area. The German supremo opted for Operation Michael. Three German armies would strike against the British Third and Fifth Armies between Arras and La Fère, on either side of the St Quentin to Amiens road. Ludendorff concluded that this was where the British were weakest and thus where a breakthrough could be achieved swiftly. The decisive stroke would be a rapid swing north-west from the Arras sector, cutting off the British from their principal supply lines and isolating the French.

February–March

At the beginning of February, 'Kaiser Bill' was in a more confident, if not arrogant mood about the prospects for 1918. Following the

The German Offensives of 1918

Russian débâcle, he was certain that Germany was once more capable of anything. At Homberg, on 2 February, the Kaiser announced to his inner circle that 'We will fling the English out of Calais' and that he had already given orders to march against St Petersburg and overthrow the nascent government of 'Socialists'. Georg Müller noted that: 'We have entered the sabre-rattling period once more'. Threats to invade Russia as an act of hubris due to local difficulties in securing the full terms of the Brest-Litovsk Treaty to Germany's advantage were, of course, ludicrous, given that Ludendorff and Hindenburg had already shifted the bulk of the German Army in the East to the Western Front. Despite the diversion of trouble in Russia, the momentum was picking up for final agreement and planning for the great offensive against the BEF in March.

There was a surreal atmosphere for those who moved in influential circles in the major cities inside Germany and especially in Berlin. Many young officers, excited at the prospect of being counted among the happy few who were to leave for the front to take part in the anticipated German triumph of arms, enjoyed their final days in the Reich Capital to the full. Splendid evenings were spent at balls and receptions across the City amongst the diplomatic, political and aristocratic élite. Evelyn Blücher described this mood so well after an Embassy reception in early March:

> Everyone [was] splendid, elegant, almost of another era [...] At the last moment several people had been forced to telephone their apologies because of the military situation, and I think there cannot have been anyone who was not conscious of the importance of the hour [...] At any moment the long-expected offensive may take place [...] and yet there we were, all apparently gay and careless, chattering away to one another as if we had not a single fear beyond how our guests were to get home again [...] The evening passed very quickly [...] I still feel in Byronic mood, and wonder how many of the men who were my guests last evening I shall ever see again. [I imagined that the poet] Lord Byron [may well have] provided a prophecy of today [for so many of those young men]:

Russia: 'A Little Local Difficulty' and a Potential Coup?

Last noon beheld them full of lusty life,
Last eve in Beauty's circle proudly gay,
The midnight brought the signal, sound of strife,
The morn' the marshalling in arms, – the day
Battle's magnificently fierce array!
The thunder-clouds close o'er it, which when rent
The Earth is cover'd thick with other clay,
Which her own clay shall cover, heap'd and pent,
Rider and horse, friend, foe, – in one red burial blent!

[From: 'Childe Harold's Pilgrimage', canto III – ed.]

Russia: 'A Little Local Difficulty' and a Potential Coup?

Germany's accommodation with Russia following the 'October Revolution' in November 1917 should have been an unqualified blessing for the German High Command. But Russia was to prove anything but entirely compliant to Hindenburg and Ludendorff's wishes and the little local difficulty that was experienced in the first months of 1918 was to have vital implications for Germany's odds in winning the contest in the West. General Max Hoffmann, a former vitally important aide to Ludendorff and Hindenburg on the Eastern Front and Chief of the German Staff in the East, said in January that: 'The whole of Russia is no more than a vast heap of maggots' and his observation was hardly dispelled by the extra-ordinary way in which the Russian delegation behaved during the Brest-Litovsk negotiations.

Max Hoffmann, who was Germany's senior military figure in the East, was present at Brest-Litovsk as the General Staff representative. Secretary of State Kuhlmann was the principal German negotiator and Count Czernin, 'ready to accept peace at any price', represented Austria-Hungary. The Bolshevik delegation considered the negotiations to be fertile ground for exporting revolutionary propaganda, but Ludendorff's instructions were to take no truck with a defeated enemy. Hoffmann and Kuhlmann were to persuade Russia to withdraw from Finland, Estonia, Livonia, Bessarabia, Eastern Galicia and Armenia; to cede to the annexation of Lithuania, Courland, Riga and the Baltic islands; to ensure that Poland was closely associated with German interests; to pay significant compensation to German prisoners of war and also to accept strong German influence in the management of the Russian economy. Kuhlmann wisely decided to suggest that sovereignty issues concerning the border countries should be decided by referenda, knowing full well that they were under German military protection and the pro-German authorities in each one would conform.

Unfortunately, diplomacy was still a planet unknown to the Hindenburg/Ludendorff partnership and military hubris led to serious rifts within the German hierarchy, which led to near-anarchy at a time when the German leadership had a real need to appear united and bullish.

First, Hindenburg took umbrage at Kuhlmann's proposed solution and, misreading the latter's intention, complained bitterly and publicly that the army was being betrayed by a Government pursuing a peace founded on reconciliation, rather than strength. Kuhlmann's negotiating skills were not only questioned but also dismissed as toothless without proper military input: i.e. that of Hindenburg himself. He told Kuhlmann that from now on he, Hindenburg, 'must have a greater influence and the definite right to approve all suggestions and decisions'. Everything, word-by-word, was to be endorsed personally by the Commander-in-Chief.

But Hindenburg had missed the point, as he was convinced that Brest-Litovsk was in session to resolve purely military matters, apparently oblivious to the vital importance of national foreign policy and the complex nature of detailed drafting and settlement of the Treaty.

Meanwhile, Hindenburg's 'Quartermaster General' Erich Ludendorff was on the prowl in the House Committee of Foreign Affairs, briefing its members that Russia was a thoroughly beaten enemy, that the Entente Allies would soon be brought to their knees on the Western Front, that Germany had no further need of allowing for the sensibilities of her own allies or neutral countries, and that stringent military demands had to be made in the East to prepare Germany for the almost inevitable war that would follow against Russia once more.

The New Year had barely begun, but a destructive storm was brewing in Berlin, which would further limit the Kaiser's influence

Russia: 'A Little Local Difficulty' and a Potential Coup?

and demonstrate the childish petulance of the man who was to be most remembered for the 'Great German offensives in the West' in 1918. On 2 January, prior to a routine Imperial Crown Council meeting, the Kaiser spoke to Hoffmann and in the ensuing discussion mentioned the question of the Polish frontier. Hoffmann judiciously recommended that Germany secure a limited annexation, for, as he explained, the last thing Germany needed was the sole responsibility for a huge territory (populated by at least two million Polish citizens) to govern and secure. The Kaiser agreed enthusiastically and announced this in the council meeting as if was his own idea. This announcement lit the short fuse to explode Ludendorff's arrogance. Ludendorff and Hindenburg then committed the cardinal sin of openly insulting their Emperor by loftily saying that they were unimpressed by such interference in a purely military affair. Immediately after this appalling affront, Ludendorff stormed out of the room, slamming the door as he went, like a spoilt child. Such behaviour would have raised eyebrows amongst his peers, but such a deliberate act of defiance and temper in front of a head of state was unforgivable.

Ludendorff caused even greater consternation at the Kaiser's Court and amongst the German 'chattering classes' when he offered to resign. Ludendorff was conceited enough to believe that the Kaiser could not sack him, as he had publicly announced that his resignation had been forced on him by his Emperor's lack of confidence in him. It was hubris of the highest order and, in effect, treasonable.

Crown Prince Rupprecht of Bavaria expressed his revulsion at the direct and public political meddling by Ludendorff and Hindenburg, but they continued to press home a number of demands, including the replacement of Cabinet Chief Valentini with a pro-Ludendorff & Hindenburg right-wing politician called Berg. At the Kaiser's residence, Georg Müller noted that: '[Berg] was an effective representative of the "H-L" company'. Crown Prince Wilhelm told 'H & L': 'You cannot demand of my father that he dismisses a statesman every five minutes just because you don't like him.'

Worse was to follow, although at first it seemed to be a triumph. On 16 February 1918, after much stalling by the Leon Trotsky-led negotiators for the Brest-Litovsk Treaty, the provisional Russian Government was told that the armistice between the two countries

The German Offensives of 1918

was at an end and that German 'police actions' would follow. It was quite a 'police force': no less than fifty-two German divisions were launched on 18 February against an already crumbling 'revolutionary' Russia. The German forces swept all before them.

Within a week the Russian Government had capitulated and agreed to swingeing terms to secure peace. The result, on 3 March, was the Brest-Litovsk Treaty.

The harshness of that treaty was bad enough, but as the moment of victory for the German military leadership passed it was soon evident that Brest-Litovsk might actually tip the balance in favour of the opposition on the Western Front. Extraordinarily, over a million German troops, including the bulk of the German Army's cavalry units, were to be tied down in Russia after all and not join the great offensive in the West.

German Plans: Russian Humiliation and Victory in the West

By the beginning of March 1918, Ludendorff had three and a half million men, or 194 divisions, on the Western Front. Sixty-seven of these were concentrated between Arras and Saint Quentin, outnumbering the British by nearly three to one. But Ludendorff knew that such numerical advantages had not borne success in the past. Previous offensives had relied on massive, protracted artillery bombardments, designed to destroy enemy defences and thus enemy resistance. They had all failed. He realized that only novel attack methods would enable Germany to achieve victory.

Following the positive signs at Riga, Caporetto and Cambrai, the supreme command of Ludendorff and von Hindenburg had faith that the guarantor of swift victory was the use of specially trained soldiers, as stormtroops, backed by well drilled and potent attack divisions alongside locally overwhelming artillery bombardments. The artillery preparation was characterized by short, concentrated barrages to the very depth of the enemy defences, behind which stormtroops would attack the enemy trench lines. They aimed to bypass centres of resistance, and break through into the enemy rear areas. Here they would destroy headquarters, communications sites, and neutralize the enemy artillery.

The BEF's Response: Defence in Depth?

The stormtroop detachments were supported by specially selected and mobile field artillery units and, in their wake, 'assault units' consisting of infantry, machine-gunners, trench mortar teams, engineers, more field artillery, and ammunition carriers.

As well as being trained to help exploit the success of the stormtroop units, they were practised in attacking strongly defended positions. They would also repel enemy counter-attacks. No obstacle should hold them up for long. Speed was paramount.

By exploiting success in this way, Ludendorff believed that the German offensive would develop an irresistible tide and achieve the elusive breakthrough.

The BEF's Response: Defence in Depth?

On the other side of no-man's-land, Haig and his generals faced 1918 with little of Ludendorff's optimism. Given the exhaustion of their troops, he and his Allies knew there was little choice but to hang on until the Americans could make a decisive difference to the course of the war. To repulse a likely German offensive, Haig realized he needed to develop a new defensive system based on depth. The defensive system was broadly similar to that of 'Elastic Defence-in-Depth' adopted by the German Army on the Western Front in early 1917. The BEF version is described in the Hampshire Regiment's Official History (based on contemporary War Diaries, letters and memoirs) thus:

> The new British Defence System involved three zones, a 'Forward Zone', held by a third of the infantry of a division; a 'Battle Zone', usually about two miles back, where the main resistance was to be offered, and a 'Rear Zone' about as much further back, to be held if the Battle Zone was penetrated. The pioneer battalions were for the most part assigned to the division's Rear Zone.

The 16th (Irish) Division was typical of the BEF units preparing the new defensive system in anticipation of an almost inevitable German onslaught in early 1918. The Irish Division, supported by the 11th Hampshires as the divisional pioneer battalion, was deployed

The German Offensives of 1918

between Epehy on its left flank and the village of Ronssoy on its right, with Villers Faucon and Tincourt, to the rear. The division was part of the British VII Corps, which was responsible for a sector of the line east of the town of Peronne. The three divisions of the corps, namely 9th (Scottish), 16th (Irish) and 21st Division, would face eleven German divisions, overwhelming artillery, mortar and machine-gun fire and a thick fog on 21 March. The strength of their newly prepared defences would prove to be the difference between survival and annihilation on that approaching, fateful day.

Field Marshal Sir Douglas Haig planned to adopt the German system that had so frustrated his troops at Passchendaele. The defences would be made up of a 'Forward Zone', or 'blue line', lightly manned, but with various strongpoints to blunt the initial attack; the 'Battle Zone', or 'red line', where the main fighting would take place; and finally the 'Rear Zone', or 'brown line'. British artillery, heavy machine guns and infantry counter-attacks, on the 'brown line', would ultimately halt any German attack that got this far.

But Lloyd George's brake on British reinforcements being sent to France meant that Haig had fewer men than a year earlier. It made it very difficult for him to put his plan into practice. Worse still, the British had been forced to take over an additional 15 miles of the Allied Front from the French. Not only did this increase the pressure under which Haig was labouring, but it also placed him in a dilemma. He had to decide if he could risk weakening the line at any point to compensate for the extra frontage he had to defend.

The British sector that would bear the brunt of the *Kaiserschlacht* in March and early April had the Third Army, commanded by General Sir Julian Byng, facing the German Seventeenth and part of the Second Armies along the River Scarpe, Vimy Ridge, Arras and the Flesquières salient near Cambrai in the north – and the Fifth Army, commanded by General Sir Hubert Gough, in the region of the River Somme. Gough's Fifth Army had taken over the extension of the British front handed over by the French. Field Marshal Haig had to spread his resources more thinly than he had hoped and, in anticipation of Ludendorff's offensive, decided he could not afford to reinforce Gough by much. Fifth Army was therefore left to do its best to build its new defences in a desperate race against time.

Eastern Treaty and a Reason to Fight on – for Both Sides

If ever a treaty made it abundantly clear why a nation should fight on against an ascendant enemy, Brest-Litovsk was the touchstone. On the Eastern Front a formal end to hostilities was reached on 3 March 1918 at Brest-Litovsk. The final treaty here between Germany and, by then, Communist Russia, demonstrated precisely what peace on Germany's, and in particular, Ludendorff's terms would mean.

Under its conditions, Russia was forced to give up one-third of her population, 50 per cent of her industry and 90 per cent of her coal production. Brest-Litovsk was punitive, overreaching and evil in its intent. Anyone who has put hand on heart since and said that the First World War on the Western Front was futile is unlikely to have realized the significance of Brest-Litovsk. If Ludendorff's 'Grand Plan' for 1918 had succeeded, a similar 'Treaty of Paris', or, dare one suggest, 'Versailles Treaty' would have formally stripped France and Belgium of their assets.

The BEF – Spoiling for a Fight?

Back on the Western Front, the BEF in particular was recovering from the disappointments of 1917, with Passchendaele and the reverses at Cambrai after such spectacular beginnings still fresh in their minds. The experience of 1917 had changed the British soldier to some extent. Perhaps there was a greater fatalism; the old camaraderie had gone. One man remarked: 'There was still comradeship, but not the homely comradeship of the past.'

Those who were part of the desperately overstretched Fifth Army found the French defences they took over to be in poor condition, which placed an almost intolerable burden on them. General Sir Hubert Gough's defences were the least developed in the British line.

Snatching the brief periods of rest they were allowed whilst out of line, the British troops hoped that when the German attack came they would not be in the trenches. Conversely, those manning the front line hoped that they would be at rest. Nevertheless, they did have faith, now, in their ability to match the German soldier. There was an innate belief that they were gaining the upper hand against the Kaiser's men and that, despite the sacrifice, they would ultimately beat them in the field. The discouraging factor was when? To many the war seemed

The German Offensives of 1918

timeless, eternal; and now they knew that they would have to endure a German onslaught and further sacrifice if they were to bring the German war machine to a halt.

Haig, facing the awful responsibility of repulsing what he knew would be a massive offensive when it came, put his faith firmly in his God and in his men. He firmly believed that the British soldier's traditional patience, endurance and fortitude would see him through what was set to be the sternest test of the war. His faith in the men of the BEF was well-founded, for they had stood and passed the test of courage and skill many times before. Even in this relatively novel experience of preparing for a defensive battle, their spirit was in no danger of breaking with men like Tasmanian Lieutenant Fred Bethune. Commanding No. 1 Section of the Australian 3rd Machine Gun Company, he was well aware of the desperate fighting in which he and his men were likely to take part and issued orders that would not only have put a ramrod in most soldiers' spines, but also anticipated Field Marshal Haig's later 'Backs to the Wall' special order of the day rather neatly. Bethune's instructions left no doubt in his men's minds what contribution they were expected to make in stemming the German assault when it came:

1. This position will be held, and the Section will remain here until relieved.
2. The enemy cannot be allowed to interfere with this programme.
3. If the Section cannot remain here alive it will remain here dead, but in any case it will remain here.
4. Should any man through shell-shock or other cause attempt to surrender he will remain here dead.
5. Should all guns be blown out, the Section will use Mills grenades and other novelties.
6. Finally, the position as stated will be held.[5]

He and thousands of other men of the BEF would soon have the opportunity to prove their doggedness and confirm whether they would be capable of passing the sternest test that they had ever endured against a revitalized, well-trained and motivated enemy.

An Omen for the 'Great Offensive'?

An Omen for the 'Great Offensive'?

On 19 March, the Kaiser was at Spa. Two days later he would be bound for the front line, or as near as he would be permitted to go, to review his troops near St Quentin. The general feeling within the Kaiser's Court was one of tension, but anticipation of a great victory. Not everyone was quite so upbeat. Georg Müller noted:

> A rainy day. Bad for the offensive planned on the Western Front, where it is raining all along the line. [It seems that] only His Majesty maintains that it is a good thing because it will keep the enemy pilots grounded. [But] one cannot help but think of our offensive at Verdun two years ago which the rain hindered so disastrously.

The Final Days ... and Hours

As March wore on there was an eerie sense of inevitability: the troops on both sides of the wire knew the planned offensive in the West was about to be unleashed. During the five nights preceding the offensive, most of the German manpower earmarked for the onslaught was brought up under the strictest security. The bulk of the artillery had been drawn up close to their firing positions prior to this, in order to correct ranges, but without revealing the massive increase in the number of batteries across the attack Front.

The stormtroops and attack divisions, after a number of weeks of intensive training, arrived in their assembly areas after marching to their positions under cover of darkness. During the day, they were kept out of sight in woods and villages. At night, whether on the march or bivouacked, troops were strictly forbidden to show any light or use fires for cooking. German aircraft were used to not only mask the move up of so many men, guns, mortars and supplies but also to ensure that these rules were strictly obeyed, reporting any misdemeanours from the air so that action could be taken to douse the lights and punish the culprits. The thousands of guns and mortars, as well as ammunition parks, supply dumps and vehicle/horse-drawn convoys were concealed in woods and elaborate efforts were taken to camouflage them.

Edwin 'Valentine' Kühns, who moved closer to the front around the Flesquières salient shortly before the attack, was amazed by the unbelievable sight of a seemingly endless stream of his comrades moving forward and the general cheerfulness of those who were about to put their trust in God and their Generals once more:

> The big offensive is now ready. All the villages near the front are full of troops. Troop movement is on a massive scale [...] Everywhere, one sees that things are going to happen in the next few days. On the 15th of March four of us [...] took 20 minutes to get through the straggling village of Laurcourt to take over the Telephone Station. This is in a dugout [...] With so many soldiers here, they have to sleep outside. Absolutely everywhere is crammed with troops.

Most of these troops were infantrymen who had trained for the forthcoming battle and now moved to their forward assembly areas a few days before the onslaught began. *Feldwebel* Max Schulz of 46th Infantry Regiment noted that:

> The whole regiment was paraded in Cambrai and our commander addressed us. He told us that we were going to take part in a great attack, that this would be the last big battle and that it would be decisive. We trusted our generals then and believed what he said. Our morale at that time was very high [...] and yet I still prayed that God would bring me safely through it.

Then, on the evening of 20 March, more than 6,000 guns and over 3,000 mortars were slotted into place just behind the 40-mile front and the assaulting infantry made their final move forward into their jumping-off positions. It seemed to most German troops involved that this time they really would prevail. The planning, the training and the self-assurance, all of which had been considered down to the last detail, gave them faith in their commanders and their own comrades with whom they were about to go over the top. In cramped dugouts and trenches, as the final hours, then minutes, ticked away there was time for reflection. One German officer noted in his diary as he prepared for this final, 'decisive' push:

21 March: *Sturm Auf!*

It is strange to think of these huge masses of troops now silently waiting and praying for our great adventure. It seems that all Germany is on the march and tomorrow, at last, we shall move irresistibly westward.

At every level from army to regiment and battalion there was a 'Special Order of the Day' passed to the men awaiting their fate to inspire them and put steel in their spines. Gunner Herbert Sulzbach was with his battery near St Quentin. His regiment received such an order on the evening of the 20th March, which he transcribed. It read:

After years of defensive action on the Western Front, Germany is moving to the attack; the hour eagerly awaited by every soldier is approaching. I am certain that the Regiment, true to its history, will enhance its reputation in the days which lie ahead.

This great objective will call for sacrifices, and we shall bear them for the Fatherland and for our loved ones at home.

Then forward, into action! With God, for Emperor and Fatherland!

Finally, as Zero Hour approached, the crews of the field guns, the 'heavies' and the thousands of mortars deployed across the whole attack front loaded their first shells and mortar bombs and stood ready for the order to fire.

It was now or never. Now was the time for Ludendorff's bold but high-risk decision to end the war with a winning last throw of the dice. He knew more keenly than anyone else at this eleventh hour that his plan had to unfold as a stunning success, which would guarantee victory, or be forever remembered as a desperate gamble that failed and threw the Fatherland into a deep and blood-soaked abyss.

21 March: *Sturm Auf!*

At precisely 0440 hours on 21 March 1918, Ludendorff struck. A total of 6,423 guns and 3,532 mortars opened fire on the British defences in Northern France. The barrage fell over a 54-mile front from the River Scarpe in the north to the River Oise in the south. In the north, von Below's Seventeenth Army was poised to attack simultaneously

The German Offensives of 1918

with von Marwitz's Second Army on either side of the Cambrai, or Flesquières salient. The much vaunted Eighteenth Army, under General Oskar von Hutier, would attack from St Quentin in the north to the Oise. General Sir Julian Byng's British Third Army faced elements of both the Seventeenth and Second Armies, and Sir Hubert Gough's severely stretched Fifth Army now faced part of the German Second and the whole of the Eighteenth Armies.

When the inferno of the massive artillery bombardment began, the initial effects were devastating. The British defenders were at first dazed by the sudden ferocity of the bombardment and then blinded, reaching out desperately for their gas masks as the German guns poured both poison gas and high explosive into the British positions. As the bombardment continued, Ludendorff's *Sturmtruppen* began to cut gaps in their own barbed-wire defences in final preparation for the attack.

At precisely 0840 hours (0940 German time) the first waves of assault troops rose from their jumping-off points and advanced, irresistibly at first. *Leutnant* Ernst Jünger later noted that:

> The great moment had come. The fire lifted over the first trenches. We advanced [. . .] The turmoil of our feelings was called forth by rage, alcohol and the thirst for blood as we went forward [. . .] to the enemy lines.

At first, it seemed that nothing would resist this human tidal wave as it began to storm through Haig's defensive lines. The German barrage moved forward 100 yards every two to three minutes, protecting the advancing men. Some British strongpoints, bypassed by the storm-troops, continued to fight on until they were overwhelmed. The British guns also fought back until they were overrun or forced to withdraw by the speed of the German advance.

Through the Red Mist

But the bitter, desperate fighting during the German assault was not without incidents of compassion on either side. Jünger, fired up by this long-felt desire to sweep away the enemy, pressed on ahead of his unit and suddenly discovered that he was on his own. Then:

Through the Red Mist

I caught my first sight of the enemy. A figure crouched, wounded apparently [...] in the middle of the pounded hollow of the road. I saw him start at the sight of me and stare [...] with wide-open eyes as I walked slowly up to him holding out my revolver [...] Grinding my teeth, I pressed the muzzle to the temple of this wretch, whom terror now crippled, and with my other hand, gripped hold of his tunic. With a beseeching cry, he snatched a photograph from his pocket and held it before my eyes [...] himself, surrounded by numerous family [...] I forced down my mad rage and walked past.

Through the thick fog and preceded by the leading stormtroop units, forty-three German assault divisions of Second and Eighteenth Army had risen up and attacked the British Fifth Army sector, and a further nineteen divisions of Seventeenth Army assaulted the British Third Army sector.

The British defenders were outnumbered and severely hampered by the impenetrable fog and deep-ranging heavy artillery fire. Many of the British artillery batteries were destroyed by German counter-battery fire or their gun crews were neutralized by the debilitating effects of gas shells. The British Forward Zone of defence quickly fell apart in places.

The short but massive bombardment and the extensive use of gas shells within the Bruchmüller artillery fire plan left the ground relatively uncratered and assisted the initial German attacks and especially the infiltration tactics of the stormtroops. The heavy mist, choking gas and breakdown in communications, as HQs were hit and telephone cables destroyed, added to British confusion.

The conditions masked the German advance as planned and the fog made it virtually impossible for many of the British strongpoints in the Battle Zone to support each other with interlocking machine-gun fire and vital artillery shoots into the mass of German assault troops.

Typically, though, a pattern of extraordinary defence was to emerge where the forward British defences were not entirely destroyed, and it was to cause immense frustration, as well as admiration, among the German troops storming forward, for the German High Command and the Kaiser.

Georg Bruchmüller

Georg Bruchmüller was a significant figure during the 1918 offensives as an innovative master of the use of artillery. Born in Berlin in 1863 within a middle-class family, Bruchmüller was commissioned into the German Foot (or Field) Artillery in 1885. He established himself as his career progressed as an expert in artillery tactics and siege warfare and was to become a renowned and highly respected instructor of artillery methods to junior German officers. However, he came close to being an unknown figure on the First World War stage when he was invalided out of the German Army as a result of poor health in 1913.

Oberstleutnant (Lieutenant Colonel) Georg Bruchmüller was persuaded to return to active duty by the German General Staff towards the end of 1914 as the war on the Eastern Front expanded. He was posted to the Artillery Staff of 86th Infantry Division, of the Eighth Army.

For much of the war, artillery was utilized for lengthy preliminary bombardments prior to infantry offensives in an attempt to destroy or neutralize enemy defences. This method had, at best, mixed results and any element of surprise was generally lost because of the clear indication that a protracted and intense bombardment was a sure sign for both sides that a major assault would follow.

Bruchmüller reviewed this method and concluded that short, concentrated 'hurricane' bombardments would have a greater effect in neutralizing the enemy defences before an offensive and thus provide the elusive, but vital element of surprise. The artillery and mortar barrage was planned to range across the whole of the enemy defensive area, rather than following the generally accepted pattern of the inflexible 'fixed' bombardment that concentrated on an enemy front and second line of defence, as well as longer range 'counter-battery' (CB) and interdiction fire. Bruchmüller also advocated the extensive use of mixed high explosive (HE), gas and smoke barrages, which exacerbated an enemy's lack of command and control under such an artillery onslaught.

Honed on the Eastern Front, Bruchmüller's methods were demonstrated with great effect in March 1916 during the Battle of Lake Naroch, and at Riga in September 1917. His innovative approach was so revered by the German High Command and the Kaiser himself that he was awarded the prestigious Pour le Mérite following the victory at Riga.

Through the Red Mist

Transferred to the Western Front in time to take part in the planning and conduct of the German counterstroke at Cambrai at the end of November 1917, he was promoted to *Oberst* (Colonel) in March 1918 and became the lynchpin for the novel modus operandi employed for Ludendorff's great offensives, for which he is best remembered. His methods earned him the nickname 'Durch-Bruchmüller', which is a neat pun on his name, translated as 'breakthrough (German: *Durchbruch*)-Müller'.

He retired for a second time soon after the Armistice and spent much of the remainder of his life as a military historian and adviser on artillery techniques. He was promoted to the rank of *General Maior* (Major General) in August 1939 on the retired list and died in Garmisch-Partenkirchen in 1948.

As an example, on the morning of 21 March, 'Manchester Hill' redoubt, overlooking St Quentin, was defended by elements of the 16th Manchester Regiment (the Manchesters) of 30th Division (Fifth Army, XVIII Corps), along with units from the 30th Battalion MGC and brigade trench mortar battery. The Manchesters were commanded by Lieutenant Colonel Wilfrith Elstob DSO MC. Elstob had been commissioned from the ranks in 1914 and had fought on the Somme, at Arras and Ypres. Highly regarded, and with both a DSO and MC as testament to his courage, his orders for the defence of the position were unequivocal. He was reported to have declared before the German attack that: 'The Manchesters hold this hill and we shall all die to hold this hill.' In short, Elstob expected his battalion to defend the position, with Manchester Hill at its heart, to the last man. The Manchesters had a rifle company in the Forward Zone, a company in the nearby village of Francilly Selency and the remainder of the battalion defending the redoubt, where Elstob's HQ was also deployed.

As anticipated, the early morning fog obscured the view from Manchester Hill and German assault troops infiltrated the Forward Zone and Francilly Selency defences before launching a major onslaught against Manchester Hill itself. The Manchesters under Elstob's leadership were true to their CO's order and held on against increasing odds as men were killed or severely wounded rather than surrender.

The German Offensives of 1918

Finally, German field guns were brought up to blast the redoubt over open sights prior to a final assault to overwhelm the few remaining Manchesters. This was carried out and the Manchester Hill redoubt fell at around 1630 hours.

Colonel Elstob was apparently killed after declining the offer to surrender, and despite a search for his body, it was never found. He is immortalized alongside thousands of other officers and men posted as 'missing' during Operation Michael on the Pozières Memorial. His VC citation noted:

> For most conspicuous bravery, devotion to duty and self-sacrifice during operations at Manchester Redoubt, near St Quentin, on the 21st March, 1918. During the preliminary bombardment he encouraged his men in the posts in the Redoubt by frequent visits, and when repeated attacks developed controlled the defence at the points threatened, giving personal support with revolver, rifle and bombs. Single-handed he repulsed one bombing assault driving back the enemy and inflicting severe casualties. Later, when ammunition was required, he made several journeys under severe fire in order to replenish the supply. Throughout the day Lieutenant-Colonel Elstob, although twice wounded, showed the most fearless disregard of his own safety, and by his encouragement and noble example inspired his command to the fullest degree. The Manchester Redoubt was surrounded in the first wave of the enemy attack, but by means of the buried cable Lieutenant Colonel Elstob was able to assure his brigade commander that 'The Manchester Regiment will defend Manchester Hill to the last.' Sometime after this post was overcome by vastly superior forces, and this very gallant officer was killed in the final assault, having maintained to the end the duty which he had impressed on his men – namely, 'Here we fight, and here we die.' He set throughout the highest example of valour, determination, endurance and fine soldierly bearing.

Despite this and many other examples of bloody-minded resistance, Ludendorff and Hindenburg's plan did appear to be carrying all before it in the south, and the situation already looked promising for General Oskar von Hutier's Eighteenth Army, where Fifth Army had only recently taken the front line over from the French. Within hours, the German drive had slipped beyond the Battle Zone and threatened a breakthrough in the British III Corps area. The right flank of General Sir Hubert Gough's Fifth Army was forced back and then withdrew under fire to the Crozat Canal.

The excellent progress of Eighteenth Army masked the frustration of both Second and Seventeenth Army in the centre and north of the attack sector. In the Cambrai sector, the plan to cut out the strong defences of the Flesquières salient by flanking attacks failed, leaving subsequent German units exposed to enfilade fire. The leading assault units of von der Marwitz's Second Army were unable to break through the British Battle Zones and von Below's Seventeenth Army was held up by the well-prepared and immensely stronger defences of General Sir Julian Byng's British Third Army.

Nevertheless, by the end of the day, a total of fifty German divisions had engaged in one of the most dramatic days of the whole war. The dazed but courageous men of General Sir Hubert Gough's weakened Fifth Army had been thrown back by the sheer magnitude and shock effect of the German storm that had blasted them since dawn.

In a similar fashion to Lieutenant Colonel Wilfrith Elstob at Manchester Hill, 2nd Lieutenant Edmund de Wind, a former Private in the Canadian Corps, but since commissioned and posted to the 15th Battalion, Royal Irish Rifles (RIR) was responsible for the defensive position known as Racecourse Redoubt, south-east of Grugies.[6]

Racecourse Redoubt straddled a railway line that led into St Quentin and was one of fourteen redoubts in the area. They had been established because of the thinness of the defensive line, and in fact there was a group of three in this Forward Zone, each held by one of the three divisional brigades. 'Racecourse' was in the middle of the three and the 15th RIR occupied it, together with the 1st RIR.

The German assault on 21 March closed rapidly with the line of British redoubts in this sector and most were immediately surrounded and cut off. However, despite mounting casualties and dwindling ammunition supplies, many of these redoubts were held for much of the first day by incredible feats of gallantry and 'last stands' by men such as de Wind and his fellow officers and men, who knew that death or capture were the only certainties. As the day progressed, and the thick fog began to clear, the Royal Irish riflemen took a toll of the German attackers with rifles and machine guns.

The Germans pressed home their attacks and most of the remaining redoubts were overrun. By late afternoon only desperate hand-to-hand fighting saved Racecourse Redoubt. Then Edmund de Wind was hit by German fire for a third time and he fell mortally wounded. Immediately after his death the remaining men in the garrison surrendered. The citation for Edmund de Wind's VC read:

> For seven hours he held this most important post, and, though twice wounded and practically single-handed, he maintained his position until another section could be got to his help. On two occasions with two NCOs only he got out on top under heavy machine-gun and rifle fire, and cleared the enemy out of the trench, killing many. He continued to repel attack after attack, until he was mortally wounded and collapsed. His valour, self-sacrifice and example were of the highest order.

Thirty or so survivors (including Headquarters Staff) were ordered by the Germans to remove their boots and were marched off barefoot into captivity.[7]

Corporal John Sayer of the 8th Battalion, Queen's Regiment (part of 17th Brigade of 24th Division), was defending a sector of the line just north-east of the village of Le Verguier, which lay just inside the Forward Zone, with the front of the Battle Zone skirting the village to the west. On 8th Queen's right flank was the 3rd Rifle Brigade, with the left flank protected in part by 1st Royal Fusiliers. The 72nd and 73rd Brigades occupied the main 24th Divisional defence to the rear of 17th Brigade.

When the German attack was launched on 21 March the British defences to the south of the divisional front were soon overwhelmed and to the north the Germans broke through the Forward Zone but were met with heavy fire from the 3rd Rifle Brigade, which was positioned in Cookers' Quarry, and with fire from the 8th Queen's.

The Reckoning

The enemy advance was stopped and no more attacks were made until early evening, when the Quarry fell and the Germans – frustrated by not being able to capture Le Verguier – began to attack the ground to the north and south of it. Eventually the village, which stands on high ground, was cut off. Corporal Sayer and the rest of his battalion would spend a sleepless night as both sides licked their wounds and prepared for further bloody action the following day.

The Reckoning

In the event, and despite numerous tales of heroic last stands and derring-do, 21 March was a disastrous day for Haig's BEF. It was the bloodiest day of the First World War. There were over 78,000 casualties, almost 40,000 on each side. Though the *Sturmtruppen* had advanced in one or two places up to 10 miles by the end of the day in the south, overall, 21 March was a day of great sacrifice and confusion.

Most vexing for the German High Command would be the fact that, although the total casualty figures were around 40,000 each, the British included no less than 21,000 prisoners and the remainder comprised 7,512 killed and 10,000 wounded: a subtotal of just over 17,500. This compares with just 300 German prisoners, but a massive 10,000-plus dead and 28,778 wounded: a subtotal of almost 39,000 killed or wounded. It was a haemorrhage of manpower that Ludendorff could not possibly sustain.

Added to this, after the events of 21 March unfolded, Ludendorff had to contend with the reality and frustration of only partial success. Less than a quarter of the first day's objectives had been achieved, and at great cost. Furthermore, the unexpected achievement by von Hutier's Eighteenth Army in the south led Ludendorff down a fatal 'garden path'. Ever the opportunist, and never the strategist, he would reinforce the southern thrust and send it bowling across the Somme countryside on a one-way ticket to nowhere of any tactical, operational or strategic consequence. The subsequent events of the spring offensives would dramatically prove the point that: 'German strategy, both in peace and war, has always been opportunist, and concerned with looking for weak places rather than with formal objectives.' [British Official History, 1918]

The German Offensives of 1918

Fog on the Somme

The early morning fog across the battlefront was a major ally for the German assault troops, obscuring the view and fields of fire of the British machine-gunners, artillery observers and battalions manning the forward Battle Zones. There is little doubt, as events would prove a week later when Operation Mars was launched near Arras, that a clear day would have had a disastrous effect on the German offensive on 21 March. Martin Middlebrook's excellent study of the first day of 'Kaiserschlacht' emphasizes that without the fog that morning:

> German infantry casualties [. . .] would have greatly exceeded the 40,000 men actually killed and wounded [. . .] and the German advance would have been halted in most places in front of the Battle Zone [. . .] The second phase of the battle would then have started under conditions much more favourable to the British.

'The Results of the Offensive are not Very Satisfactory for the First Day'

The fact that *Kaiserschlacht* – the Kaiser's battle – had begun without the stunning success expected was reflected at Supreme Headquarters:

> 21st March 1918: Left Spa at midnight [. . .] Arrived [at the front] at 9.20 a.m. [. . .] His Majesty left immediately by car with a small escort for Avesnes, which Hindenburg had chosen as his Headquarters for the offensive [. . .] After lunch we drove in the direction of St Quentin to the 1st Guards Division in billets at the village of Essigny. Lightly wounded men were on their way down the line [. . .] Back in the train at 7 p.m. [. . .] The results of the offensive are not very satisfactory for the first day. [We were told] after supper that the British had taken a terrific pasting. Actually, the day's objectives were not reached.

Either way, the die was cast. Germany's 'Great gamble in the West' was under way and her fate now rested squarely on the shoulders of General Erich Ludendorff.

22 March: Ludendorff 'Chops a Hole' to Break Through

The German tide continued to break across the British defences and further stormtroop units and attack divisions were thrown into battle. Operation Michael was making progress, especially in Fifth Army's sector, but in the north, hard fighting and well prepared BEF defences continued to frustrate Second and Seventeenth Armies.

Back in the British 24th Divisional sector, where Corporal John Sayer was holding out with 8th Battalion The Queen's, there had been little respite since the fighting the day before. At 0400 hours on 22 March, the German attacks were renewed and here the first objective was to capture (finally) the village of Le Verguier. Early morning mist and dim light were in the Germans' favour. The 8th Queen's and the 24th Machine Gun Battalion held on desperately against incessant assaults, artillery, mortar and machine-gun fire from three sides. However, by midmorning there was no choice but to withdraw to a more defensible line or surrender. Most of the remaining men of the battalion and machine-gun crews were able to withdraw, assisted by the mist, which now gave them cover against the enemy for once.

John Sayer chose to stay alongside other men in his company to protect those who were falling back via Le Verguier. He held the flank of an isolated post for two hours. Although the enemy was extremely close to his position he was protected by the thick mist and managed to repel a series of attacks and inflict heavy casualties. Leading a charmed life at that time, he managed to repel all German attempts to overrun his position until most of his men were killed or wounded. Inevitably, he was hit too and seriously wounded. Soon afterwards he was captured with the few survivors of yet another heroic defence.[8]

Crucially, though, this action – and many like them – had imposed a frustrating delay on German progress: 8th Queen's and the remainder of 24th Division had held Ludendorff's troops in check for over twenty-four hours.

Nevertheless, overall, the 22nd marked a further deterioration in the plight of Haig's increasingly pressed BEF in Third and especially Fifth Armies. An uncharacteristic misunderstanding between the normally reliable and tenacious Lieutenant General Sir Ivor Maxse, commanding XVIII Corps, and Fifth Army commander, Sir Hubert Gough, led to a rather hasty withdrawal of his own troops to the River Somme and a subsequently forced retirement by the neighbouring XIX Corps on his left to conform. Equally, from a broader perspective, Third Army's right flank was exposed by the increasingly fragile position of Gough's left flank and also the apparent destruction of the Fifth Army units in the south under the continued pressure of Oskar von Hutier's Eighteenth Army onslaught. General Sir Julian Byng, commanding Third Army, was perhaps ill-advised to delay the evacuation of the Flesquières salient as it became increasingly vulnerable after a most heroic defence there on 21 March. Sadly, this not only led to the needless sacrifice of many 2nd and 63rd (Royal Naval) Division personnel, but also led to a wider gap between Third and Fifth Armies.

Meanwhile, OHL could not disguise its disappointment of the attacks across the front as a whole, even though the 'flanking' Eighteenth Army was ripping through Gough's Fifth Army in places and making greater progress than the main assaulting armies to the north. Imperial disenchantment was equally evident:

> 22nd March: The mood at breakfast was low. We must reckon with the possibility that the offensive might come to a standstill. The High Command was blamed for their undue optimism.

23 March: 'A Beautiful Morning ...'

Despite the apparent gloom in the German camp early on the 22nd, the 23rd dawned as if some great and decisive shift had occurred as a result of progress the day before. Flushed by the apparent triumph of arms against the BEF, the Kaiser was in a particularly buoyant mood throughout day three of his offensive – the 'Kaiserschlacht' or 'Emperor's Battle'.

On the morning of 23 March, Hindenburg accompanied him on a trip as close to the front as he could be allowed to go, to visit his own triumphant troops and also to review some of the thousands of British prisoners. At St Quentin, where the first shots were fired at dawn on the 21st, he addressed a column of unkempt, tired BEF men in English and with perhaps surprising respect: 'Well, gentlemen, you have fought very bravely, but [...] God is with us!' *Gott mit Uns* – every German soldier wore a belt with a buckle stamped with those three words, and many would die for the Fatherland and the Kaiser between March and November 1918 with that faith still intact.

Already, the German press was trumpeting 'Triumph in the West' and in an aggressive, quasi-religious and utterly dismissive manner. The target was 'England', not France, and the 'copy' heaped contempt on the island race. For example, *Germania* blasted:

There can be no period of peace [. . .] in the world until the presumptuous notion that the Anglo-Saxons are the 'chosen people' is defeated. We are determined to force with the sword the peace which our adversaries did not see fit to confide to our honest word.

The *Deutsche Zeitung* went further:

Away with the miserable whimpering of those people who even now would prevent the righteous German hatred of England and sound German vengeance. The cry of victory and retaliation rages throughout Germany with renewed passion.

On the Home Front the unfolding situation was creating an almost surreal wave of relief and a previously scarce-imagined notion that, with Russia already out of the war, this great offensive in the West might be, at last, the victory promised so many times before only to be unfulfilled. But such anticipation and excitement were invariably qualified by the thought of what had gone before and the cost, whether in triumph or disaster. Englishwoman Evelyn Blücher wrote in Berlin that:

The great offensive has begun, and the newspaper headings all speak of a great German victory. The whole [of Berlin] is being flagged and the bells are ringing [. . .] I hear some of the remarks made by passers-by and, shall I confess it, for the first time since the outbreak of the war I am beginning to doubt [the British ability to survive this onslaught] – and wonder if it is [actually] possible that the Germans can reach Calais? [. . .] It is a beautiful morning; one of those spring days when the world seems to be young and strong and full of hope in the night. The flags are flying from the housetops; the branches of the trees are waving in the wind and the high white clouds hurrying by, as if carrying the news of the great battles to other lands. The day looks as if it were rejoicing, but Nature is always callous to human suffering, and who can think of rejoicing, whether friend or foe, when such horrible suffering is being inflicted on mankind?

The 23rd did show promise, true enough. As the day wore on it became increasingly clear that von Hutier's Eighteenth Army was opening up a serious gap in the British line. At the Kaiser's Court and amongst some of the senior German commanders the mood swung dramatically from disappointment on the progress of the first and second days to wild optimism about the imminence of a crushing and decisive victory.

But this was also a fateful day in the course of Ludendorff's strategy – and so soon after *Kaiserschlacht* had been let loose.

A Change of Heart – and Direction

By 23 March, much of Hubert Gough's beleaguered Fifth Army had been pushed back over 12 miles and General Oskar von Hutier's Eighteenth Army was pressing westwards to seize potential crossings of the important Crozat Canal and large areas of the Somme sector. Ludendorff was seduced by the prospect of further success here, so unaccountably allowed the merely tactical opportunity that was opening up (as a result of von Hutier's comparative progress) to deflect him from his original declared strategy to strike north-west with the bulk of his Second and Seventeenth Armies further north. Instead of strengthening the right flank to guarantee the successful wheel in that direction, he reinforced von Hutier's forces and issued new orders, which ordered the Seventeenth Army to strike towards St Pol and the Second Army west to take Amiens.

In detail, von Hutier, originally given the principal mission to provide flank protection for the other army groups, was to now thrust south-west towards Noyon and Montdidier in a more clearly defined effort to split the BEF from the French. It was a decision that would have far-reaching consequences, as, rather than pressing forward as

A Change of Heart – and Direction

a coherent, cohesive mass west and then north-west against the British, Ludendorff had single-handedly demonstrated his naivety on a fundamental principle of war – namely, 'concentration of force'. Instead of keeping all of his assault force in line and together for the anticipated 'big left hook' in order to unhinge the BEF's defences, Eighteenth, Second and Seventeenth Armies would hereafter advance in divergent directions, creating huge gaps across each other's flanks and stretching the already hard-pressed logistical support behind each army to its absolute limit.

Ludendorff's inspiration and opportunist streak had led to orders that were largely based on his and his Staff's false assumption that Haig's commanders and men facing the onslaught across the attack front were already close to capitulation, which was by no means the case, although the crisis for the BEF was still very real.

To the north of the Fifth Army struggle, German efforts were renewed against the British Third Army. In particular, 47th (London) Division, as part of V Corps, was deployed to the Flesquières salient on 19 March – and it was the right flank division of Third Army and on the left flank of Fifth Army. As it happened, from 21–23 March, the 'Londons' were responsible for defending the right flank of one army and maintaining some contact with the extreme left of Fifth Army's defenders. By the evening of 22 March, Fifth Army's battle had left its left flank exposed and 47th Division had to cover a yawning gap. The Divisional History noted that:

> The 16th (Civil Service Rifles) Battalion, on the extreme right, had an anxious and heavy task to perform, and the fact that no Germans filtered through the gap throws great credit on the way in which patrols and machine-gunners did their work [that night].

That evening, the division had conducted a skilfully executed night withdrawal to the Third Defensive Line.

At dawn on the 23rd, most of the 15th Civil Service Rifles Battalion occupied half-dug trenches along the line of Dessart Ridge Switch, just north of the Metz–Fins Road and south of Havrincourt Wood. The position was some 10–15 kilometres due east of the Somme battle-field of 1916 around Delville and High Woods and the villages of Les

The German Offensives of 1918

Bouefs, Ginchy and Guillemont. The division was in a difficult and unstable position, with the majority of the Civil Service Rifles occupying the precarious flank and facing south to account for the fact that no other British or Dominion unit was in touch because of Fifth Army's apparent disintegration at that time. Trouble was expected soon – and the Londoners were not disappointed. The enemy in V Corps' sector were principally from 21st Reserve and 16th Reserve Divisions. After early skirmishes, German probing led to the discovery of the huge gap that had opened on 47th Division's right flank and it proved an irresistible opportunity for the leading battalions of 16th Reserve Division.

From midmorning, the German assault troops began to swarm into the gap, setting up machine guns and mortars to enfilade D Company on the right. Artillery fire compounded the problem and German shells had greater effect against the makeshift trenches dug by the London troops overnight or in the early hours of that same morning.

The Civil Service Rifles were hanging on and were determined to disrupt 16th Reserve Division's efforts to bypass and then encircle them, but this was to prove a forlorn hope. Suddenly, the battalion's left flank was almost turned when men of B & C Companies witnessed a large number of British troops withdrawing in disorder on the battalion's left. The Commanding Officer, Lieutenant Colonel W. H. E. Segrave, his adjutant and an *ad hoc* group of 'the 15th' stemmed this tide and the retreating soldiers were rallied and formed into a defensive flank, facing east. Nevertheless, as the German shelling increased, other battalions on the Civil Service Rifles' left began to withdraw under intense pressure and the German assault battalions were strong enough to not only press home their attack against the retiring troops, but also detach sufficient men, machine guns and mortars to let fly at the Civil Service Rifles' left flank also. By noon, the battalion was dangerously exposed across Dessart Ridge, and when Lieutenant Colonel Segrave gave the order for the remnants of the battalion to conduct a fighting withdrawal at around 1400 hours, D Company was completely surrounded.

D Company's brief but dogged last stand gave the rest of the battalion chance to move back in better order, as some of the local German attackers were focused on winkling D Company out of their

54

positions, rather than pressing home the attack on the rest. It also reflected the extraordinary courage of British and Dominion men who were facing impossible odds across the entire German attack front in these early days of the *Kaiserschlacht*.

The German attack was fierce and ultimately every man of D Company was killed, wounded or cut off until taken prisoner, wounded or not. Private Walter Humphrys, who had only recently been promoted to No. 1 in a Lewis Gun team, and whose gun team occupied the last position on the right flank, recalled after the war that:

At 2.30 p.m. [*sic*] we, D Company, were given orders to charge the German machine guns as the only chance of getting out. I don't know who gave the order but it was a toss up as to whether it was a wise thing to do or not. We went over the top to try to break through without any covering fire and we were pretty much wiped out before we got halfway. The few still standing crawled back into the trench, which the main body of the Germans attacked at around 4.30 p.m. [*sic*]. Finish!

The time between the brave but hopeless charge and 'Finish' was about two hours, but enough for the Germans to baulk at the idea of an immediate and decisive assault against the pitiful number of surviving D Company men and thus provide further time and space for the remainder of the Civil Service Rifles to fall back in a more disciplined manner than might have been possible. Walter Humphrys graphically explained what those last hours prior to his capture were like:

When I got in the trench there was another man – a big fellow [...] I was crouched behind him looking over his shoulder when I heard a 'ping' and I saw a bullet come out from behind his ear. The thing had gone through his tin hat and he didn't move. He couldn't have been conscious of it at all, absolutely gone in a split second. Later [...] I heard a lot of shouting from the German side and I popped my head up quickly and saw three lines of Germans coming down on the trench, so I scrabbled up the other end of the trench to see if anybody was up that end. I found about half a

The German Offensives of 1918

dozen men. We waited until [the Germans] were right on top of us and then we gave ourselves up [...] They were quite reasonable and didn't rough us up at all, but just passed us down to the people behind.

Sadly, although Walter and most of his fellow captives from D Company were to survive the experience of remaining as POWs for the rest of the war, their company commander, Captain Middleton, was captured but later died of the wounds received during the heroic but doomed last stand that afternoon.

For those who had managed to retire in reasonably good order, there was to be a twenty-four-hour period of incessant mobile warfare, which demanded entirely different tactics. The 47th Divisional History acknowledged that:

From now on [...] the task of the Division was not to hold definite positions to grim death, but to keep the enemy's advance in check, and at all costs to prevent him striking in behind us, thereby cutting off our troops and subsequently rolling up the flank of the Third Army.

Unwittingly at this stage, the Civil Service Rifles, in common with other 47th Division battalions, were applying novel tactics in an intuitive way to achieve precisely what was required. This was not the mark of a beaten and disorganized rabble of demoralized BEF soldiery that so many historians, journalists, playwrights and other literary people have accused the troops of being at this time. The 47th London Division was pretty typical of the determined, courageous and well-led fighters that would prove that defeat was not an option in their book – and that the flame of possible German victory would be well and truly snuffed out in the days, weeks and months to come.

The Civil Service Rifles' CO, Lieutenant Colonel Segrave collected a group of around fifty men and held a ridge line about three miles back, allowing other groups to withdraw beyond them, until they too were forced to retire as dusk fell. The CO and his remaining company commanders or other officers placed in temporary command, decided to order the remnants of the battalion to split into small parties and

A Change of Heart – and Direction

work their way back to support positions some three miles further back, around the village of Le Transloy. Naturally, the venture was fraught with difficulty and in places it would be a case of every man for himself. Despite this, and the fact that many wounded men had to be left behind that night and that the exfiltration was done at night, many did make it.

There is no official account of the battalion's fighting withdrawal and exfiltration, although the War Diary picks up again in recording that at 0900 hours on the 24th at least 150 men were assembled under Col Segrave in the support position near Le Transloy. There were over 300 casualties confirmed by the roll-call, although it was already clear that well over 50 per cent of these were likely to be 'prisoners of the Kaiser', as was later to be proved the case. Some, of course, were not captured but died of wounds or drifted back to British lines at a later date. Nevertheless, it would be months before the fate of every man would be known.

Individual acts of initiative, boldness and sheer bloody-mindedness were the root cause of the German respect and admiration for the fighting spirit of an enemy so woefully underestimated by their own commander, Ludendorff.

Lance Corporal Charlie Amsden was to win a DCM in actions that reflected another angle to the brave but doomed final stand of Walter Humphrys and his fellow machine-gunners in D Company. Amsden commanded another Lewis Gun detachment and took on waves of German 16th Reserve Division assault troops to help cover the Civil Service Rifles' withdrawal as the remainder of his detachment were killed or wounded to a man. Undeterred, he kept the Lewis Gun in action, taking up several firing positions as the retirement developed and forced the enemy to go to ground on a number of occasions after many of their comrades had fallen victim to Amsden's steady, accurate fire. Eventually, he became separated from the rest of the battalion, but found another battalion on the night of 23/24 March and was one of the men who rejoined the remnants of his own battalion the next morning.

With fewer than 200 fighting men at his disposal the CO continued to command a spirited, though much depleted battalion and over the next twenty-four hours they would occupy and withdraw from no less than four hasty defensive positions and their withdrawal would take them back across the battle-scarred landscape of the Somme 1916 fighting, including High Wood, which the 47th London Division had captured in another bloody battle around eighteen months earlier.

An Evening with the Kaiser

As the Civil Service Rifles were preparing to withdraw to their former Somme positions without the plucky men of D Company on the evening of 23 March, the German High Command at Supreme HQ was in the mood for celebration and most were jubilant, believing that the *Kaiserschlacht* was close to its promised success. However, Admiral Georg Müller, who tended to have his finger on the pulse of reality and 'Realpolitik' within the German leadership circles, noted in his diary:

> His Majesty returned from Avesnes [Ludendorff and Hindenburg's forward HQ] bursting with news of our success. To the guard on the platform he shouted as the train pulled in: 'The battle is won, the English have been utterly defeated.' There was champagne for dinner. The communiqué was read telling of our great victory under the personal leadership of His Majesty the Emperor (a well-meaning lie crafted by Hindenburg and Ludendorff), which the German people will not believe for one moment.

The generous accolade by Hindenburg and Ludendorff may well have been prompted by the ecstatic Kaiser's gesture in decorating Ludendorff with the Iron Cross with Golden Rays for the victory that he believed was at hand. It was, incidentally, the first time that it had been awarded for more than a century to Marshal 'Vorwaerts' Blücher after his timely intervention on the evening of the Battle of Waterloo.[9]

But though the British Fifth Army had been sorely pressed and Seventeenth and Eighteenth Army had scored notable successes, the decisive breakthrough still eluded them. Despite the Kaiser's great optimism, *Kaiserschlacht* was by no means at an end, let alone won.

24 March: Allied Perspective

By 24 March, the assault divisions involved in *Kaiserschlacht* had forced the British line to withdraw up to 15 miles. By now, 50,000 prisoners were in German hands, together with hundreds of artillery guns. Peronne had been abandoned on 23 March, and Bapaume was to fall into German hands on this day, which meant that the offensive would now push west across the Somme 1916 battlefield towards Albert.

Gough planned a bold counterstroke for the 25th using four brigades from General Maxse's XVIII Corps and a new French 22nd Infantry Division to regain the Somme line at Pargny, which was approved at the highest level, but was destined to fail on 25 March when it was met by a major assault around the Nesle/Ham bridgehead by the German IX Korps.

The situation in the north and in proximity to the Third Army flank was a good deal more serious for most of the day than on the Somme. Lieutenant General Congreve's VII Corps, with the 9th (Scottish), 21st and 16th (Irish) Divisions in the van, was forced to withdraw up to 6 miles whilst continuing to maintain a tenuous link with Byng's right flank. Further heroic last stands helped Congreve and his divisional commanders effect the retirement in reasonably good order. Most notably, the South African Brigade of 9th Scottish Division, with less than 1,000 men holding the line just north of Marrières Wood,[10] stood firm for over eight hours against continuous attacks by battalions of both the 199th and 9th Reserve Divisions until their last rounds were fired and virtually every Springbok was at least wounded. The Brigade commander, Brigadier General Dawson, and no more than 100 troops finally surrendered, but held their heads high as they soon learned that their defence had cost Ludendorff's men at least an eight-hour delay in this sector, as well as guaranteeing that other battalions and brigades of VII Corps had broken off the fighting and withdrawn to fight another day.

Meanwhile, by the time the other divisions of VII Corps reached a more defensible line, each brigade was reduced to barely one battalion's-worth strength (of around 650–750 men total) and every man in the line or in the corps, divisional and other headquarters throughout Congreve's command was utterly exhausted. The line held

The German Offensives of 1918

was well inside the old 1916 battle sector, between Albert in the north and Bray-sur-Somme and the River Somme in the south. Congreve's corps was reinforced there by the 35th Division from Flanders and a 1,000-strong contingent of the 1st Cavalry Division.

At 2000 hours Field Marshal Haig visited Julian Byng to underline the vital need to hold the Arras and Scarpe sector and maintain a link with Gough's Fifth Army. He also told him that Third Army would soon receive a number of reserves to boost his defences. Shortly after 2300 hours, the French C-in-C, Henri Philippe Pétain, visited Haig at Dury. Haig was told that Gough would come under the broad command of General Fayolle, commanding the Groupe d'Armées de Reserve, as French troops had by now taken over almost 15 of the 36-mile Fifth Army Front. Pétain was, according to Haig, 'very much upset, almost unbalanced and most anxious' and he was obsessed by the fear that even at this stage, the main German blow would be delivered in Champagne, rather than unfold here. Haig was then staggered to hear that largely as a result of this concern, Pétain had told Fayolle that very afternoon to be prepared to cover Paris by falling back on Beauvais if the main German thrust continued to head south-west as von Hutier's Eighteenth Army appeared to be doing.

Finally, he handed over his order of the day stressing that French integrity was vital and, by making little reference to Anglo-French liaison, rather gave the impression that he was prepared to abandon the BEF to its fate if necessary. Haig pressed him on this matter and Pétain confirmed that if Paris was threatened the BEF's right flank and the chance of significant French reinforcement elsewhere along the British sector would be left to hang in the wind. The thoroughly pessimistic Pétain then told Haig that: 'It was the only thing possible' if Ludendorff's offensive 'compelled the Allies to fall back farther still.'

Field Marshal Sir Douglas Haig was furious but kept his counsel. He returned to GHQ at Montreuil and at 0300 hours on 25 March cabled London, warning that: 'If General Ferdinand Foch or some other determined General who would fight was not given supreme control of operations the BEF would [have to] fight its way slowly back covering the Channel Ports.' Haig then wrote personally to French PM Georges Clemenceau and Foch deploring the threat by Pétain to abandon the BEF if he thought it expedient and, to prove his point, urging that the French despatch at least twenty divisions to assist the BEF's efforts in stemming the German tide.

It was a vital few hours – and Haig's selfless and broad understanding of the action required after Pétain's dire performance was to bring much-needed coherence to Allied strategy within forty-eight hours.

24 March: German Perspective
By the evening of 24 March the German Seventeenth, Second and Eighteenth Armies had all enjoyed success to some degree, even though the original 'flank protection' – namely von Hutier's Eighteenth Army – continued to make the most spectacular progress, thanks to Ludendorff's intervention. It was the onslaught that would mark the public perception of the German offensives for generations of historians, students and commentators to follow: i.e. that the *Kaiserschlacht* led to the Germans advancing 40 miles into British territory; but with the distinct impression that this gain was 'across the whole attack Front' of all three German armies involved and that it had an ultimately successful purpose. Neither was true, of course, as subsequent events would show.

25 March: Ludendorff's 'Strategy' Altered Once More
On the 25th, Ludendorff sent out revised orders, which reversed those issued two days earlier, shifting the main emphasis of Operation Michael back to the German centre and right, where Second and Seventeenth Armies had stalled.

Regardless of the extraordinary survival of 47th London Division and others like them over the past few days, the BEF's fate did still hang in the balance. Apart from Gough's ill-fated counterstroke, which came to grief against the German IX Korps, led by *Generalleutnant* von Oetinger, thrust into the Nesle–Ham bridgehead, 25th March was one of mixed fortunes on both sides. The two French divisions sent to augment the Fifth Army attacks were driven back in disarray for the most part and were pushed back over 2½ miles during the day's fighting, which forced the more determined British units to pull back to conform.

The German Offensives of 1918

Lieutenant General Butler's British III Corps sector between Ham in the north and Noyon in the south was put under the French Third Army commanded by General Humbert, which brought four Infantry divisions and a dismounted Cavalry division into the line together with the remnants of the 14th, 18th, 58th and 2nd Cavalry Divisions of III Corps, plus the newly arrived British 1st and 35th Infantry Divisions.

Despite this apparently strong force, III Corps was short of ammunition and artillery support and was all but overwhelmed by *Generalleutnant* von Conta's IV Reserve Korps, whose 33rd Division grasped the opportunity to outflank Noyon from the west in the gap between the British right flank and French left. At 1730 hours, a strong company-strength of 170 men from 18th Division's 54th Brigade carried out a tremendous local counter-attack and retook the village of Babouef in less than thirty minutes, killing or capturing 230 astonished German troops, took ten machine guns and ammunition and also saved a French field battery from almost certain destruction, and then held on as a rearguard until well after midnight before withdrawing.

Lieutenant General Watts' XIX Corps near Peronne was to become the only cohesive Third Army corps and stood alone on a 13-mile front astride the Somme, a couple of miles apart from Third Army to the north and Maxse's XVIII Corps south. The German 208th Division of General von Hofacker's LI Korps had to fight hard against elements of 8th and 24th Divisions to force crossings at Eterpigny and Biaches. Von Hofacker's other main assault division, the 19th, spent most of the day in an epic struggle against 8th Division attempting to take and cross Brie bridge. After almost twelve hours they succeeded, but with heavy losses. British casualties, however, were equally high. The 2nd Middlesex lost almost 75 per cent of its strength before what was left either slipped away or was forced to surrender. XIX Corps began to withdraw to semi-prepared positions some 4 miles to the rear at around 1630 hours under General Watts' orders. It was achieved by the early hours of 26 March.

On Third Army front, VII Corps had another relatively good day on the Albert–Bray defence line – stiffened by the newly arrived 35th

25 March: Ludendorff's 'Strategy' Altered Once More

Division – and held off five separate German Second Army divisional attacks, inflicting heavy casualties on each occasion.

The V Corps was severely depleted and could provide a mere 1,000 men per brigade to take on a series of German assaults from dawn to dusk to the east of Bapaume. Under these attacks, which were supported by infantry guns, rifle fire and machine guns only, the depleted British 17th, 63rd RN and 47th London Divisions pulled back in good order to the old Somme lines, but inflicted huge casualties on the German assault divisions.

The 47th London Division occupied a strong position along Contalmaison Ridge just south of the Albert–Bapaume road. Here they threw back another determined German attack, which was enough to take the stuffing out of the German Reserve Division troops assaulting yet another British defensive line after a continuous but slow and exhausting advance in the same period. They did not press home the attack and by then some of the assault battalions were well below 50 per cent strength anyway.

General von Below's Seventeenth Army struck Lieutenant General Harper's British IV Corps with fifteen divisions on either side of Bapaume. Most of 19th (Western) Division's 2,500 survivors were attacked by the best part of six German divisions for over ten hours, although they were forced back onto 51st Highland Division's line near Loupart Wood by early p.m. The 42nd and 62nd Divisions were brought in to boost the corps defences, but the struggle continued against a tenacious German assault well into the evening.

On a filthy night of rain, hail and biting winds, thousands of stragglers were found and somehow brought together before 19th Western Division and the remainder of the corps were withdrawn to a line behind the Bucquoy–Albert–Bray line. At 2100 hours, Third Army received the New Zealand Division from the Flanders area and the Kiwis were allocated to IV Corps in the area of Mailly–Maillet west of the River Ancre.

Some semblance of order was restored after some of the heaviest fighting so far. There was no doubt that the German assault divisions had suffered heavy casualties, but the momentum and initiative still appeared to be with Ludendorff's men.

The German Offensives of 1918

26–27 March: The Allied Crisis Comes to a Head

The town of Albert fell after brief fighting on 26 March. In less than a week, the German Second Army had managed to advance across the ravaged Somme battlefield and make significantly more ground than had been lost in 1916. General Byng's Third Army was compelled to pull back its right flank in order to conform with Gough's Fifth Army's left flank, while standing firm around Arras and on Vimy Ridge. Field Marshal Sir Douglas Haig was now much more alive to Gough's plight and the potential danger to the vital railhead and Main Supply Route centred on Amiens.

Haig, therefore, had become doubly alarmed at what he felt was inadequate support from his pessimistic opposite number, General Henri Philippe Pétain, who feared that Ludendorff was still likely to launch a fresh offensive against the French sector and the Chemin des Dames in the Champagne area in particular. Pétain had already declared that if necessary he was prepared to withdraw south-west to Beauvais, away from the BEF, to guarantee the security of Paris. Pétain had a point – after all, he was certain that if the German breakthrough did occur, Haig's armies would pull back towards the Channel Ports and thus leave the French to fend for themselves or go under.

Doullens: Allied Response and a Shift in German Fortunes

The ambivalent attitude of doubt then optimism amongst the German leadership as the *Kaiserschlacht* tide swept on were not reflected by the British and French High Command. Both Haig and Pétain knew that the British were in trouble, and Haig was already rushing reinforcements from the northern sector of his front to plug the gaps in his defences.

Haig believed that only French assistance could guarantee that the desperate, though determined, efforts of his men to prevent a German breakthrough would succeed. Contrary to the tales of many historians who suggest otherwise, Haig recommended that a 'battle conference' was held to consider and agree on a joint Anglo-French response to the German onslaught. He duly met his French counterparts on 26 March at Doullens. As a result, Marshal Ferdinand Foch was appointed as the Allied Generalissimo. Although Foch's authority was limited, his appointment did at least end the dangerous independence of the national commanders, ensuring closer co-operation between them, which undoubtedly strengthened British and French resolve.

The consensus at Doullens would not solve all the Allied problems overnight: the German Eighteenth Army would continue to make further progress for a few days more, and force the French out of Montdidier, but Foch's optimism gave the Allied commanders a real psychological boost and, while French reserves did take time to arrive to reinforce their BEF colleagues, there was no longer any doubt about the French commitment to help protect Amiens and stiffen the British defensive lines.

On the same day, as the Allied cause was seriously debated and solutions found in principle to the crisis in hand, the humour was quite different in the Kaiser's headquarters. Admiral Georg Müller wrote in his diary:

Once more His Majesty returned from the front with brilliant news, so that we all drank champagne once more. Spirits were so high that His Majesty declared that if an English delegation came to sue for peace it must kneel before the German standard for it was a question here of a victory of the monarchy over democracy.

ANZAC Interlude

When Old John Bull is threatened,
By Foe on Land and Sea,
His Colonial Sons are ready,
And at his side will be.[11]

The deteriorating situation across the front for the BEF – and Fifth Army in particular – led to rapid moves from areas such as the Ypres salient and Armentières sectors to the Somme for Dominion troops such as the Australians and New Zealanders of the ANZAC Corps. On 26 March, a brigade of the Australian 4th Division closed a gap at Hébuterne, north of Albert, and the New Zealand Division also pushed the German line back between Mailly–Maillet and the infamous 1916

The German Offensives of 1918

Somme battlefield sector, Serre, Redan Ridge and Beaumont Hamel. With the exception of the 1st Division, the AIF was then brought in to plug yawning gaps and hold on to the front line astride the Somme river between Morlancourt and Villers-Bretonneux, which was due east of the threatened and vital town of Amiens.

During the next month units from the 4th, 3rd, 5th and 2nd Australian Divisions would help stem the German attacks in the area of the Somme from Hébuterne in the north to Hangard Wood and Villers-Bretonneux ('Villers-Bret') in the south. As was common during much of the German offensive effort against the BEF between March and the end of April, the fighting in which the ANZAC troops engaged was confused, with units from various divisions detached to particular areas as each emergency reared its ugly head. The combined courage of both Aussie and British troops would be crowned by the heroic defence of 'Villers-Bret' and Hangard Wood, in the south, in both early and late April.

The German perspective of the fierce and gruesome struggle that had been raging already across the Somme, Ancre and Cambrai/Arras sectors was summed up unwittingly by Signalman Valentine Kühns, who had been serving in the Cambrai sector since mid-1917:

On 25 [March], we returned to our Company in Haynecourt. There our worn clothing was replaced [...] On 26.3 [sic], at 1 p.m., the advance began again [in our area] via Bourlon, the road to Anneux and then the main Cambrai–Bapaume road [...] Behind the sugar factory in Graincourt, on the canal, was the first English [defensive] position [...] All along the road were dead soldiers – up to Bengny nearly all ours, after that those of the English. [Most] were lying in the ditches, their faces covered by a thick layer of dust, heads bent slightly forward, crouching, some still carrying their packs and wearing their helmets. Nearly all of them had their shoes or boots taken away and their packs rifled for valuables [...] Some of the bodies looked ghastly. For example, [there was] a German soldier whose eyes and cheeks had been gnawed by rats. Others were naked, others with broken skulls.

27 March: A War Machine Driving 40 Miles to Nowhere

The 27th was perhaps the zenith of the German effort during *Kaiserschlacht*. On this day the Kaiser, Hindenburg, Ludendorff and the senior staff at OHL believed that the desired breakthrough was within reach. On the face of it, the achievement – so often quoted by those who imagine the German spring offensives of 1918 as the whisker away from victory – was extraordinary. In less than a week, Operation Michael, part one of the *Kaiserschlacht* proper, had punched a hole up to 40 miles deep into British territory.

But this great leap forward, the like of which had not been seen since 1914, was illusory. The successes had been most evident in the south and this was where Ludendorff had reinforced to exploit it.

There is no question that the front-runners in the 'Hindenburg Stakes' were advancing up to 40 miles beyond the front line that existed until the early hours of 21 March. In most places north of von Hutier's most successful penetration of the British line, the assault had gained 15 miles at most, and achieved much less in the northern sector of the Somme region. Here, the full effects of the devastation caused by Ludendorff's insistence on a 'scorched earth' policy during the withdrawal to the *Siegfried Stellung*, or Hindenburg Line, a year before had come back to haunt the German assault troops as they struggled to establish any real momentum across such blasted terrain.

It was entirely as Crown Prince Rupprecht had predicted at the time, and senior commanders were only too aware that Ludendorff's hubris had been the root cause. In the southern sector of the Somme, where von Hutier was pressing ahead, the German successes were partly on account of a relatively poorly prepared Fifth Army defensive network and the fact that the ground was not as badly scarred as in the German Second Army's assault sector. Furthermore, the 40 miles gained were in the wrong place: for the direction taken was to the south-west and not the sweeping wheel north-west, which was Ludendorff's original intention.

In the real world, Ludendorff could not hope to sustain this advance anyway because of the poor logistic tail that had struggled since the first day to sustain the ravenous demands of the German infantry and artillery as it pressed forward. The stormtroop units had no integral logistic back up and relied on ammunition, food and water from the resupply of the attack divisions behind them. Logistic support across 40 miles of devastated countryside was a virtually impossible task for the German logistic units, as they lacked sufficient motorized and horse-drawn transport. On top of this, many of the transport columns that were organized and despatched towards the forward battle areas were regularly forced to run the gauntlet of bombing and strafing by Allied aircraft.

In addition to the massive logistical problems that existed, Ludendorff now had another fundamental flaw in the plan to contend with: how to exploit tactical success. He could not do it with either cavalry or tanks. Only nine tanks were used on 21 March – and five of those were captured British Mk IVs. Only seventeen of the lumbering German A7V tanks were built and their size (33 tons), crew of no less than eighteen men and 'cross-country' speed of around 2 miles an hour, rendered them virtually useless anyway.

The cavalry divisions were mainly on duty in Russia. As a result, the giant cracks in Ludendorff's assertion that strategy would take care of itself if the tactics worked were being exposed. As John Terraine later commented:

> As the year would show, the days of cavalry as an arm of exploitation on a modern battlefield were over; yet, feeble as it was, the cavalry was the only exploiting arm that existed. [For the Germans] to launch an offensive intended to win the war with none at all was not just foolish: it was criminal.

Turning Tide

Although it was not yet apparent, the tide was turning against Ludendorff. By the fourth week of March 1918, the British had been severely battered by the German offensive. But Ludendorff had not yet achieved his declared aim: complete breakthrough and the destruction of the British resolve to fight on.

On 27 March, the French Reserve Army, under General Marie-Émile Fayolle, to the south of the continued thrust into the guts of General Sir Hubert Gough's Fifth Army, faced thirteen divisions of General Oskar von Hutier's Eighteenth Army. Von Hutier's attacking force had four rested divisions and was well-supported by field and medium artillery. Fayolle had ten divisions, of which two were cavalry. Despite fierce resistance along the line throughout the day, Fayolle was forced back so that the German 206th Division managed to enter the road and rail centre of Montdidier.

On that same day in the BEF sector, Fifth Army had a mere nine weak divisions against fifteen German divisions drawn from III Korps of von Hutier's Eighteenth Army and XIV Korps of General Georg von Marwitz's Second Army to the north. Only six of the divisions had been first line units on the opening day of Operation Michael.

The 27th was a clear indicator of the problems arising from British doggedness in defence and the breakdown in command and control that Ludendorff's plans had failed to take full account of, or had ignored. Such lack of foresight, based largely on a characteristically dogmatic approach, was costing the soldiers under the German High Command very dear. In an epic encounter at Rosières, south-east of Amiens, *Generalleutnant* Lüttwitz's III Korps planned to smash through the British defensive line held by Lieutenant-General Sir Herbert Watts' XIX Corps. By now, the British had learned and applied the hard lessons of the beginning of Operation Michael and the German attacks were more predictable than they had expected.

Consequently, from strong dug-in positions, field gun batteries continued to fire and hold their ground, and well-sited machine guns held their fire until the first German attacking waves were within a few hundred yards, then hit them with devastating fire. In front of Rosières, the British defenders refused to give ground, despite wave after wave of desperate German attacks. Even the élite 4th Guards Division was held up for over four hours by the 16th Irish Division, which was already weakened by the loss of 50 per cent casualties.

Von Lüttwitz's men must have been demoralized by such tenacity.

But the troops of 208th Division, assaulting Harbonnières just south of the St Quentin to Amiens road, were incredulous when their attack was stopped by the 'death or glory' ride in a counter-attack by Brigadier General E. P. Riddell, leading the remnants of his Brigade on a snaffled artillery horse. By nightfall, though some German penetration had occurred, the British line had either been restored, or a new line consolidated against further attacks. Over 1,000 German prisoners were taken, with at least the same number dead and missing – rather more than the British losses in this sector on that day.

The Remaining Cream of the Fatherland is Wasted on the Somme

German losses were higher than Ludendorff would have hoped, but most of those killed were Ludendorff's irreplaceable stormtroops. Their replacement caused a bitter response, partly because many who took their place were not fully trained for the role and partly because they actually weakened the infantry divisions that followed them into battle. This stripping of 'ordinary' units to reinforce the depleted stormtroop formations led to ever more resentment from commanders and the rank and file who remained in those units. Many complained that specialists, such as signallers, medics and transport personnel, were being transferred to front-line infantry units to make good the shortfall caused by those infantry battalions having to provide still more of the under thirty-fives for stormtroop duties.

Ludendorff's surviving troops were becoming exhausted by the intensity and unrestrained stress of battle. Also, they were running out of essential supplies such as food, water and ammunition. The shortages were already apparent, even amongst units in the rear and HQ Staffs. Signalman Edwin 'Valentine' Kühns noted in his diary in the final week of March that:

> At this time, the food got worse. [Then] on Easter Sunday, we had nothing except half a loaf of bread per man [...] Everyone was miserable, as they were so hungry. A comrade brought a joint of horsemeat from a horse that had been killed, which we had to roast, but everyone had only about a quarter of a pound. That was the first horsemeat that I had knowingly eaten. It was very tough, but it tasted good.

28 March: The Day Germany Lost the War

Still determined to achieve outright victory, Ludendorff launched Operation Mars on 28 March to trap the northern British armies by striking north-west from Arras. Operation Mars was to be the crowning

28 March: The Day Germany Lost the War

glory of the first week of the great offensive and it was designed to pull the hinges off the British defensive door, preparing the way for the German breakout and sweep towards the channel ports. The normally cautious Rupprecht had great hopes for Operation Mars, and was moved to note in his diary that: 'We stand immediately before the success of the final breakthrough.'

But Ludendorff's plans had already begun to unravel. The storm-troops were being lost against an increasingly tenacious British defence. The British and Dominion troops of Fifth and Third Armies continued to fight and to hold on. When the German bombardment lifted on the morning of 28 March and Operation Mars was launched, there was no thick, swirling mist to cover the German advance, the preparatory bombardment was not as concentrated as on 21 March, and the infantry tactics were less sophisticated.

Mars was intended to break the British defences north and south of the River Scarpe, east of Arras. The objective was to take the city of Arras and as much of the high ground to the north (including Vimy Ridge) as possible. This would be a serious blow to the British, and to the morale of the Allies. It would also secure high ground for a later offensive in Flanders, designed to sever the British lines and drive through to the Channel.

Operation Mars had never been seen as a major part of the programme of attacks and, at times, had been shelved. The German command, however, decided to go ahead with the attack and re-allocated artillery from the other parts of the front to the operation. Eight German divisions were earmarked for the initial attack, with four in support. They faced four British divisions – from north to south they were: 56th (London), 4th, 15th (Scottish) and 3rd Divisions.

The 3rd Division had been involved in the earlier stages of the German offensive and had been forced (to the chagrin of the Division's commander) to withdraw from the forward line in order to conform with the 31st Division to the south.

All of the divisions were aware that a German attack was imminent and this allowed measures to be taken to prepare. In the case of the 56th Division, arrangements were made to take troops out of the forward posts in case they were bombarded by the German artillery. In addition reserves were created from the pioneer battalion and the companies of Royal Engineers to plug any gaps that appeared in the line. In the case of 15th (Scottish) Division an *ad hoc* battalion was formed, and a similar 'Provisional Battalion' in 4th Division, including troops from the transport lines and details left behind by other battalions.

The 56th (London) Division, to the north of the line, was in the process of extending its line further to the north to take over 1,500 yards of front line from the Canadian Corps. As a result the line was stretched more thinly than previously and there was some confusion over the actual location of units. At least one company of the 1st Canadian Rifles was still in position at Sugar Post, behind the outpost line, and stayed put in order to assist their British comrades. In spite of this confusion at least one of the outposts of 56th Division was left unmanned during the bombardment and reoccupied in time for the start of the attack.

The German barrage commenced at 0300 hours, mixing gas and high explosive shells, and concentrated initially on the reserve lines. From 0400 hours the front lines were subject to intense bombardment, including trench mortar fire, and the outposts were largely destroyed by the weight of fire.

The barrage, however, appeared to be less well focused than on 21 March. Much of the fire on rear sectors was 'area fire', which was to knock out British artillery batteries, rather than counter-battery fire, suggesting that the Germans had not had time to locate their opponents. The British batteries were well established, with good observation in the north from Vimy Ridge.

The Germans started to attack at 0550 hours and, unusually, their assault did not consist of one thrust, but a series of probing moves starting in the south. The first attack was against 8th and 9th Brigades of 3rd Division, at the southern end of the line under attack. The 76th Brigade, to the north was not attacked until 0645 hours. At 0600 hours, 44th Brigade, the southernmost brigade of 15th (Scottish) Division was attacked and an hour later the other two brigades of the division faced stiff opposition.

The attack north of the River Scarpe does not seem to have started until 0730 hours. The weather was clear and 'SOS' signals were sent up as soon as the attack started. British field and heavy artillery had been relatively little affected by the German bombardment and soon found plenty of targets.

The tactics of the German divisions seems to have varied, possibly due to differing experience and preparation. In some cases large bodies of German troops were spotted forming up in areas such as Oppy Wood and these became targets for the heavy artillery, which caused huge casualties amongst the German attackers before they had even moved off.

The differing tactics may be the result of the mix of divisions used. The northern German division (23rd Reserve Division) had only recently moved to the area of Oppy Wood from the Eastern Front. Other divisions, such as 187th Division (which attacked in the 4th Division sector) and 12th Division (which attacked in the area of 15th (Scottish) Division) were better prepared and seem to have made more use of infiltration tactics.

In other cases the accounts given by the British soldiers involved spoke of the Germans advancing in large bodies, even 'shoulder to shoulder'. The 56th Division history says 'it was widely noticed by the men of this brigade that the enemy approached in a slow, dazed manner. The brigadier thinks that this may have been due to the great weight carried by the German infantry who seem amongst other things, to have carried a week's rations.'

The German bombardment had done huge damage to the outpost line and, in places, had virtually wiped out the forward companies holding them. In places the survivors did what they could do to resist the German attackers with a mix of rifle and Lewis-gun fire.

On the front of 3rd Division, the first to be attacked, some forward companies of the 1st Northumberland Fusiliers and 13th King's Liverpool were wiped out as they tried to resist the oncoming Germans. A handful managed to get back to the reserve companies who then put up a stout resistance. Although threatened by Germans working through captured trenches to the north and south they managed to establish strong defensive flanks and hold the attacks.

At one stage a company of the 1st Northumberland Fusiliers found itself fighting on three sides but it was eventually able to pull back to a more defensible line on the edge of Neuville Vitasse. Reinforcements came from the reserve battalions and the division conducted a fighting withdrawal to the Green Line, with very heavy casualties inflicted on the Germans. The Green Line held against further attacks although, because the trenches were broader and shallower, more casualties were suffered from artillery fire.

Accounts of the battle speak of 'colossal' casualties being inflicted on the attackers and a number of heroic stands and fighting retreats were carried out. Although there were numerous occasions when it looked as though the Germans had worked their way round the flanks of the defenders they were unable to break through the defences and, by evening the attacks petered out due to the losses and exhaustion of the German infantry.

To the north of the 3rd Division the 15th (Scottish) Division had been engaged in a desperate fight to hold their lines. On the right the positions held by 7th Cameronians was virtually obliterated by the bombardment and only isolated pockets were able to mount an effective resistance. Those few who survived retreated to a second line as the battalions behind held the initial German attacks and then, as their flanks were exposed, retired to the Army Line, inflicting very heavy casualties on the Germans.

The two brigades to the north were attacked later and generally held off the attackers until they were left exposed to attacks from the flank. In the north the 7th/8th King's Own Scottish Borderers managed to retain their forward positions, keeping contact with 9th Black Watch by means of a defensive flank. The position to the south, however, was becoming more uncertain as large bodies of German infantry pushed along the Cambrai road to Feuchy chapel. Although the attacks were held, and the line re-established by a successful local counter-attack, they did threaten the flank of the 46th Brigade.

A decision was taken in the late morning to withdraw to the Army Line and conform with the 3rd Division to the south. This withdrawal was carried out successfully and the line was re-established. The German attacks continued but they had suffered 'unusually heavy losses' from rifle and machine-gun fire. At one point a small group of Germans occupied the Bois de Bouefs but were driven out by a determined counter-attack by 6th Cameronians, who not only drove them out of the wood but established the basis for an outpost line to the east of the wood, together with the adjoining 13th Scots. Once again the heavy losses inflicted on the German attackers caused them to pause and they were unable to sustain any further advance.

At 1800 hours a concerted effort was made, with some success, to move the line forward and join up with the 4th Division to the north, pushing the exhausted German infantry out of some of the forward positions they had reached. The 4th Division had arranged its defences with one battalion of each brigade in the front line. Once again some of these outposts suffered severely, with 2nd Essex being severely mauled by the German bombardment and attacks. So few remained that they were incorporated into the 2nd Lancs, to their rear, but the attacks were then held by the supporting battalion.

In the centre, the 1st Battalion of the Hampshire Regiment had managed to withdraw its front-line groups from the outpost line to the strongpoint line before the Germans' assaults commenced. The battalion found itself being attacked from the rear of its left flank and had to withdraw rapidly from the battle. However, it had lost contact with the brigade to the north (where the 2nd Essex had been) and was hard-pressed by Germans attacking along the Havana trench.

A readjustment of the line in the early afternoon and the arrival of reinforcements from 1st Battalion of the Rifle Brigade allowed the line to be stabilized and contact to be resumed with the 2nd Lancashire Fusiliers on the left. Withdrawals to the south meant that a defensive flank was required to hold the line but the German attacks later in the afternoon made no further progress.

To the south of the Hampshires was the 2nd Battalion of the Seaforth Highlanders. They held an exposed Mount Pleasant position in the valley of the River Scarpe and the pushing back of the line to the north and the threat of being cut off meant that they were also forced to carry out a withdrawal to a more secure position. This was carried out successfully and the battalion was established on a new defensive position along the railway.

The biggest threat north of the River Scarpe came at the junction of the 4th and 56th Divisions. The heavy losses in 2nd Essex and heavy losses to the 1/16th London Regiment meant that, in spite of sustained resistance, they could not hold Towy Post.

Much of the front line and forward posts in this area were destroyed by shelling. A small group of about fifty Queen's Westminsters held out

A Memorable Account

A vivid tale was left by one of the few survivors of the group holding out against the German attacks. He estimated that there were five waves of German attackers, each five lines deep. Rapid rifle and machine-gun fire kept the Germans at bay for an hour, until the rifles were red hot. Fighting was at close quarters with each side using grenades to try to stop the resistance of the others. Eventually the British survivors were reduced to just three remaining grenades and, with a German machine gun established behind them, they had to conduct a fighting retreat back to the next line of trenches, silencing the machine gun on the way.

near the company headquarters and managed to hold up the German attackers, causing heavy casualties. The heavy attacks, combined with the withdrawal to the south forced the remaining Queen's Westminsters to fall back to the Ditch Post line and hold Towy Alley as a defensive flank. Unfortunately, the supporting artillery, unaware of the defenders' dispositions, managed to blow in the trench block that was stopping the Germans making further progress.

Further to the north, Mill Post – held by 1/5th London Regiment (the London Rifle Brigade) – was devastated by the German bombardment. The London Rifle Brigade had been trying to extend its line to the north during the night, as part of the general move north to take over more of the line by 56th Division.

The loss of Mill Post and Towy Post allowed the Germans to take the village of Gavrelle. But they found themselves in a hollow and were subjected to intense artillery bombardment and indirect fire from fourteen machine guns, causing enormous casualties. Meanwhile, the remnants of the two battalions, together with reinforcements from the rest of 169th Brigade, and a battalion from 167th Brigade, managed to hold the line against repeated attacks, and retained contact with 4th Division to the south.

In the north, 1/4th London Regiment held Wood Post. The post had been evacuated before the bombardment and was reoccupied before it was reached by the German attackers. The defenders took a heavy toll of the German infantry coming through a wood in small parties but had to withdraw once the nearby Beatty Post was taken, in spite of resistance from the depleted defenders – only one officer and six men returned.

Oppy Post was also taken by the German attackers, who had taken control of the whole of the outpost line. The reinforced defence of the Bailleul–Willerval line was too much for the remaining German attackers and they were unable to make further progress. At one point they did succeed in capturing two machine guns and some ground in the area held by the London Scottish (1/14th London Regiment) but they were driven out by a well-timed counter-attack.

By nightfall the four divisions were still strongly holding a line in the Battle Zone and each division was still in touch with its neighbour. Nowhere had the Germans been able to achieve a sustained break-through, other than capturing the forward trenches and outposts and causing heavy losses to the battalions holding the front-line trenches.

British losses had been heavy, with several battalions being reduced to a handful of survivors. Most of these were withdrawn on the night of 28 March, with reliefs coming from reserves and from two Canadian divisions that were moved from the north to provide support. In all cases the four British divisions had fought off repeated, sustained and often fanatical attacks. At times the position had looked very precarious but the German infantry were unable to exploit any gains that were made, especially as their tactics were, in many places, more reminiscent of the shoulder-to-shoulder German attacks during the First Battle of Ypres. Those German battalions that did attempt infiltration tactics found to their cost that they were of little value, as the British were able to maintain a continuous line of resistance throughout the day. Any stormtroop groups that did penetrate the line were easily and rapidly captured or killed, isolated from the main body of the assault battalions, which were being mauled before the British wire. The effectiveness of sustained rapid rifle and machine-gun fire, with Lewis guns doing a lot of the work, was remarked upon by many of the defenders.

In addition the artillery was in action throughout the day and not only tore gaping holes in the waves of the German attackers, but also overwhelmed the much-vaunted German guns with effective counter-battery fire. The offensive unravelled completely when the German

The German Offensives of 1918

commanders realized their field artillery – tasked to move forward to support the leading assault units – was systematically destroyed or swiftly driven off by the British gunners.

Ludendorff, quoted in a number of the battalion histories for those involved in the battle, stated:

> The Seventeenth Army had already attacked, in the last days of March, in the direction of Arras, making its principal effort on the north bank of the Scarpe. It was to capture the decisive heights east and north of Arras. The next day the Sixth Army was to prolong the attack from Lens and carry the high ground in the area. I attached the greatest importance to both these attacks. To have the high ground in our possession was bound to be decisive in any fighting in the plain of the Lys. In spite of employing extraordinary masses of artillery and ammunition, the attack of the Seventeenth Army on both banks of the Scarpe was a failure.

There were a number of reasons for the German failure in launching Operation Mars on 28 March and a few hard lessons learned. First and foremost, the offensive lacked any element of surprise and, compared with the first day of Operation Michael a week before, the preliminary bombardment was inadequate and failed to either completely demolish the British defences or put enough of the defending artillery and mortars out of action. Next, many of the German assault battalions were largely inexperienced and had not been adequately trained in the new methods, consequently many infantry units were attacking in waves that invited slaughter, rather than by fire and manoeuvre.

Worse, Ludendorff's troops frequently ran into well sited, solid and organized defences, which guaranteed further slaughter. Furthermore, the British commanders had learned from the experience of the previous seven days in other sectors that they could evacuate Forward Zone and front-line outposts, reducing the effect of the intense artillery bombardment, but then reoccupy the positions and wreak havoc on the German assault waves before they were across no-man's-land. In an uncanny and macabre parallel with the British experience of 1 July 1916, the Germans were now losing the 'race to the parapet'

Feier des 30jährigen Regierungsjubiläums des Kaisers im Großen Hauptquartier.

Zensiert
Paul Hoffmann & Co.
Berlin-Schöneberg.

1881.
phot. Bild-und Film-Amt.

...iser Bill', von Hindenburg and Crown Prince 'Willy'. *(Allen Collection)*

Sir Douglas Haig. *(IWM)*

Young German recruits in 1917: destined to fight and die during the offensives of 1918. *(IWM)*

British soldier: eighteen in 1918.
(Allen Collection)

American troops arrive in France in 1917.
(Allen Collec

Von der Westfront.
Einige Typen der ersten gefangenen Amerikaner.

Zensiert
Paul Hoffmann & Co.
Berlin-Schöneberg.

phot. Bufa
1753.

American prisoner
'at the Kaiser's
pleasure'.
(Allen Collecti

MARK IV (FEMALE) TANK

British Mark IV tank.
(Allen Collection)

German A7V tank.
(Allen Collection)

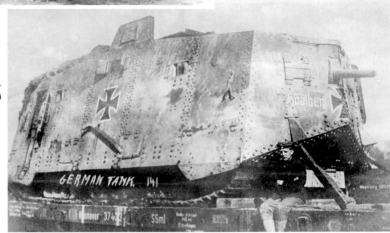

GERMAN TANK. 141

rmtroops.   *(IWM)*   A typical German stormtrooper.   *(Allen Collection)*

Salvation Army girls making pies
for the boys in the front line.
(Allen Collection)

WAACs tending graves at Abbeville, February 1918.
(Allen Collectio

FM Paul von Hindenburg and
General Erich Ludendorff.
(Allen Collection)

'Happy New Year', Christmas 1917, *Die Notenkraker*, 22 December 1917.

(Die Notenkraker)

Operation Michael: German artillery unit moves through St Quentin, 21 March 1918.
(Allen Collection)

Aus dem besetzten St. Quentin.
Deutsche Artillerie auf dem Marsch durch die Stadt.

Zensiert
Paul Hoffmann&Co.
Berlin-Schöneberg.

1587.

British prisoners of war, March 1918.
(Allen Collection)

Anglo-French co-operati[on]
March 1918.
(Allen Collect[ion])

German machine-gun crew, 1918.   *(IWM)*

'Killed in Action' by German artist Kathe Kollwitz.
(Her only son, Peter, was KIA in October 1914.)
(www.mystudios.com/women/klmno/kollwitz.html)

A German soldier provides some comfort for a wounded British prisoner. *(Allen Collection)*

The German Offensive begins to bog down. *(Allen Collection)*

Zur Eroberung des Keil- und Pöhlberges.
Minenwerfer beim Sturmreifschießen eines feindlichen Stützpunktes

Zensiert
Paul Hoffmann & Co.
Berlin-Schöneberg.

1902.
phot. Bild-und Film-Amt.

Stormtroops: trench mortar team, April 1918. *(Allen Collection)*

Defiant Brits, April 1918.   (Allen Collectio

Dead baby-faced stormtrooper, 1918. (IWM

Aussie John Barney Hines, souvenir hunter. (AWM)

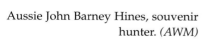

British troops of the gallant 55th Division blinded by a gas attack, April 1918.   *(IWM)*

End of the dream of victory: German assault trooper dead in a Flanders ditch, 1918.   *(IWM)*

The youth of German POWs surprised their captors in 1918.   *(Allen Collection)*

Entente Cordiale, May 1918. *(Allen Collection)*

Positions on the Aisne, held by the French against massed German attacks, May–June 1918.
(Allen Collection)

Stormtroops during Operation Blücher-Yorck, May–June 1918. *(Allen Collection)*

French poilus who held
firm against the German
onslaught of Operation
Blücher-Yorck.
(Allen Collection)

Operation Gneisenau:
machine-gun crews go
to action, June 1918.
(Allen Collection)

Aus den Kämpfen zwischen Montdidier und Noyon.

Zensiert
Paul Hoffmann & Co.
Berlin-Schöneberg.

1882.
phot. Bild-und Film-Amt

Maschinengewehre werden in einem zerschossenen Hause in Stellung gebracht.

Knocked-out German field
gun and crew, June 1918.
(Allen Collection)

Poilus who stoppe[d]
Operation Gneiser[nau?]
June 1918.
(Allen Collect[ion]

The lucky ones: German boy-
soldiers, captured in 1918.
(IWM)

General Charles Mangin, architect
of the Allied counter-offensive in
July 1918.

The Alliance: Aussie and French colonial troops fraternize near Villers-Bret, June 1918. *(AWM)*

Open warfare at last! ussie troops advance e Hamel, 4 July 1918. *(IWM & AWM)*

German prisoners of war, July 1918. *(Allen Collection)*

British Tommies wi[th]
captured German
machine guns, July
1918. (Allen Collectio[n])

Beginning of the end: raw, young
German soldier surrenders to a grizzled
Scots infantryman, 1918.   (IWM)

A great day for the BEF; a 'Black Day' for
the German Army: Amiens, 8 August 1918.

Mark of the fighting in 1918: the Australian 64th Battalion near the Hindenburg Line, September 1918. *(AWM)*

Dead German machine-gunner, September 1918. *(Allen Collection)*

American troops advance, September 1918. *(IWM)*

Barbed wire cut, America[...] creeping on the German[...] with Hand Grenades–Fra[...]

Poignant image: German
machine-gunner killed in th
last week of the war.   (IW

Ankunft der ersten Militärzüge
mit den heimkehrenden Truppen, die die Freude
und den Humor nicht verloren haben.

Arrival of the first
German military trains.
Home – and for good –
November 1918.
(Allen Collection)

German troops ret
to the Fatherland,
November 1918.
(Allen Collec

28 March: The Day Germany Lost the War

and suffering accordingly. Finally, the relative inexperience, naïve tactics and poor preparation of many of the German units thrown into Operation Mars meant that they quickly disintegrated, as each wave was mown down or left leaderless during their attacks.

By this time Haig's troops knew what to expect and were able to mow down line after line of attacking German infantry at their leisure. The slaughter was gruesome, yet the method by which the Germans attempted to advance was almost inconceivable after four years of war. British defenders recorded that:

[When] the smoke cleared [...] 200 yards in front [of our trench] were the enemy in full view bearing down on us in a compact and huddled mass [...] I counted five lines, each [...] five deep [...] In an instant [there was] the rattle of rapid fire, a fire sustained almost continuously for an hour till [our] rifles were red hot.

So, with the exception of some progress on the right flank, the grand Mars offensive proved to be an abject failure. Around Morlancourt, some of the German-held territory was actually lost to General Sir John Monash's 3rd Australian Division, just less than two years on from the infamous 'first day on the Somme'. But this time it was a German massacre before the wire and under the deadly machine guns and artillery of the British defenders.

Eyewitnesses described the fruitless German attacks:

The Germans came on time after time with the greatest bravery, sometimes almost shoulder to shoulder, each time assured that it required but one more effort to break the British front, only to be held and then repulsed by the combined force of guns, machine guns and rifles.

The assault divisions took massive casualties for little territorial gain and thousands more were taken prisoner. A follow-on assault, Operation Valkyrie, which was planned as an exploitation phase after a Mars success, was quickly cancelled. The God of War had changed sides and meted out terrible destruction on the hapless German infantry. It is significant that both the German and British Official histories do not give detailed casualty figures for this particular slaughter, for slaughter it was.

The failure of Operation Mars showed what could be done with well organized and resolute defences and this increasingly became the pattern for dealing with the German offensives. It was a real blow to German morale, as the Mars débâcle completely unhinged the plan to turn the British flank and sweep north-west and added further incentive for Ludendorff to reinforce the success of Eighteenth Army in the south where the gains were of little strategic, operational or tactical value. Most of the eight German divisions directly involved sustained enormous losses and several were reduced to limited effectiveness for the remainder of the war. In one case the estimate was that the division had lost 605 of its strength. In another case, a man from the 188th Regiment wrote: 'We tried to break through on 28 March 1918, but only pushed Tommy back to his reserve line and don't forget it was with enormous losses to ourselves.'

Loss of Life to Loss of Control

The disastrous results of Operation Mars were matched by the stench of deception that began to waft across the battlefield. The German assault troops now realized to their horror, as they overran British supply depots, that their resources were poor by comparison. Drained by continual battle, but euphoric in their achievements to date, they began to lose much of their renowned self-discipline. On the same day that their comrades were being slaughtered near Arras, many who had attacked across the former Somme battlefield of 1916 reached Albert. Lieutenant Rudolf Binding famously recalled that:

> Today [28 March] the advance of our infantry suddenly stopped near Albert. Nobody could understand why [...] Our way seemed entirely clear [and] [...] our division was right in front of the advance, and could not possibly be tired out [...] [After entering Albert myself] I began to see strange figures, who looked very little like soldiers, and certainly showed no sign of advancing [...] There were men driving cows before them on a line [...] Men carrying a bottle of wine under one arm and another one open in

their hand [. . .] Men dressed up in comic disguise. Men with top hats on their heads. Men staggering. Men who could hardly walk [. . .] When I got into the town the streets were running with wine.

Exhaustion led to ill discipline, albeit briefly, as the troops at Albert were soon ordered forward once more. But Operations Michael and Mars had failed to find the formula for the promised breakthrough.

30 March–2 April: Allied Resistance Epitomized by Australian Grit

Private Verdi George Schwinghammer was a member of 42nd Battalion, 11th Brigade of General Sir John Monash's 3rd Australian Division, AIF. Verdi was the Australian-born son of German parents and had served in 42nd Battalion since 1916. The 42nd Battalion's motto was *cede nullis* or 'Yield to no one'.

In March 1918 Verdi was with the battalion when it was sent to the Somme from the Flanders sector to stem the German tide. His diary extracts reflect the typical actions that were being fought just over a week into the *Kaiserschlacht* and reveal the true picture of Allied resolve against brave but increasingly desperate German attacks:

Easter Saturday, 30th March 1918: The nicest day we had had for over a month and the sun was shining beautifully. All the morning, things had been very quiet [. . .] The only noise was from the aeroplanes as they cruised about the skies. All the men in my section were asleep in the rough dugouts and I happened to be on duty – keeping watch in the trench.

About midday the enemy suddenly opened up on us, put down a terrific bombardment on a front of several miles – and commenced his attack.

We were all rather surprised at his audacity in attacking in broad daylight but he was evidently suffering from a swelled head owing to his previous great victory – an advance on a wide front several miles deep, capturing thousands of prisoners and much material and guns.

Of course the noise from the guns woke everyone up and there was a rush to the different positions in the trench. Our rifles were always ready for action (bayonets fixed) leaning against the parapet of the trench. In less than two minutes our Lewis guns were at work, sweeping the ground in front of our trench with bullets and as usual, our gunners in reply to our S.O.S. signals, put down a great barrage on the German positions.

The enemy did not know exactly where our front line was and the shells directed against our particular trench fell wide of the mark, but he put down a terrific bombardment on Sailly-le-Sec and the village soon became a mass of flames and a heap of ruins [...] Our trench was slightly protected by a rise in the hill and was not as exposed as other parts of the battalion front, but nevertheless bullets were whizzing around our heads the whole time that the battle was raging. From a point in our trench, the observer could see the Germans massing ready for attack. They came in mass formations to the top of the hill in front of us and then spread out into single file, shoulder to shoulder in a wave, rushing forwards towards our trenches. [However] we were holding our own and hurling the enemy back as he repeatedly made fresh attacks. When they came over the hill they were excellent targets for our Lewis and Vickers machine guns, which mowed them down like flies. About two o'clock, the battle had reached its highest, but we held on [...] At about three o'clock [in the afternoon] he made his last attack and was again pushed back.

Thereafter, just a few shells came over.

We were still in our trenches and hadn't lost an inch of ground although of course we suffered heavily and very many of our men were either killed or wounded, but the enemy losses were appalling. As the evening sun shone on the hills, one could see, even with the naked eye (but with glasses, very plainly) thousands of dead Germans strewn on the sides of the hills [...] Next day (Easter Sunday) was quiet and uneventful and I was one of a patrol party that night.

Easter Monday again broke fine and the Germans bombed our trenches from aeroplanes in daylight. They flew so low that we could easily distinguish the faces of the aviators as they peered over from their machines and on one occasion actually saw the bomb leave the plane. That night, I was again on a patrol. Our work was to go out to an unoccupied post near Sailly Laureate cemetery (which our men had dug the previous night) and see if the enemy had found and occupied it – a trap we laid for him. We crept out and when we got close to the post, lay down (with our rifles loaded, bayonets fixed, etc.) and a mills bomb in one's pocket. Stayed in this position until midnight but saw no sign of the enemy and were then relieved by another patrol [...] I was just coming off gas guard at daylight on the third morning when the Germans attacked the 5th Australian Division, who were then holding the front line. He shelled the back areas, where we were, very heavily and we had a rough time of it, and took many casualties. Several of us went along a gully which he was not shelling for shelter. (Afterwards this same gully became called 'Shrapnel Gully') [...] Just as we got there a huge shell burst about fifty yards from us, covering us with debris and mud and a fragment of the shell flew past my face and cut the top off the nose of the chap next to me.

The order now came for us to get ready to go up to the front line and reinforce our troops. [We were close to the line] [...] when we were told that we would not be required as the 5th Australian Division had pushed the enemy back without further assistance.

30 March–5 April: Amiens Remains an Elusive Prize

The gritty defence of the Somme over the final days of March and early April meant that Amiens was still out of reach, especially as von Hutier's Eighteenth Army had been encouraged to swing south-west, rather than north-west. The strategic goal had been sacrificed for tactical opportunity, but to what purpose? Much of the ground captured across the front was little more than the land devastated by the Somme battles in 1916 and the ground ravaged by the Germans themselves in their withdrawal to the *Siegfried Stellung* or Hindenburg Line, twelve months before. Von Hutier's gains were of no strategic, or even in many cases, tactical importance.

Not surprisingly, therefore, fatigue, the psychological blow of the huge losses sustained and disillusionment had all taken their toll on the

The German Offensives of 1918

German commanders and their men at the end of March. By then, most units could go no further and they were forced to go on the defensive. It had been an extraordinary week but the British, supported by the French, had held. The first crisis was over – for the Allies at least.

The extraordinary turn of events throughout this momentous seven days had not yet begun to affect the German people, although it would soon. But the individual anxiety for loved ones fighting in the West affected everyone one way or another. Evelyn Blücher was in an ideal location to observe the central hub of this activity and gauge the mood of the German hierarchy and more common, working-class German people in the Capital. At the end of March she wrote:

> Our house stands in a very central position, being in the main thoroughfare connecting two big stations: the Friedrich Strasse and the Postdamer Bahnhof; and there is always a great deal of traffic passing our windows. This morning I feel fascinated by the seemingly cheery life going on out there and stand rooted at the window, trying to escape my own sad thoughts. There are the freshly equipped troops marching away staidly and soberly enough, with the small poignant following of white-faced women trying to keep pace with their swift march. How many of them will ever see the Brandenburg Gate and the victorious figures on it again? [...] There is a newspaper-man shouting out the news that almost makes one believe that the German Army has crossed the [English] Channel. There is the flower-girl offering her small fresh bunches of violets and snowdrops to women who have no thoughts of flowers, but hurry by with anxious pale faces all in one direction [...] the Kriegsministerium (War Ministry) [...] where the fresh lists of casualties appear daily.

The German War Machine Develops
Major Engine Trouble

For Ludendorff, von Hindenburg, and the exhausted, disillusioned men under their command, the end of March brought a depressing realization that the promised swift victory – like that promised four

Cheerful Sacrifice?

years earlier – was one that may go begging. The momentum of the offensive was dependent on manpower and horsepower respectively. The lack of motorized transport made the movement of troops, weapons, ammunition (especially artillery ammunition), and other supplies more difficult between the railheads and forward positions. Even the horse-drawn transport was nowhere near as plentiful as it should have been to sustain an offensive on this scale.

Ludendorff's most precious and finite commodity, the German soldier, was the motor that dictated the mobility of the German Army throughout the offensive. The pace of the advance was thus entirely dependent on stamina and the speed of the advance on foot. Ludendorff had precious few tanks, no armoured cars and negligible cavalry, so he relied heavily on his stormtroops and attack divisions to develop and maintain the momentum of each assault. The horrendous casualties amongst the stormtroops in particular merely highlighted the differences between the élite assault units and the other divisions. Tellingly, the losses were more than a statistic to Ludendorff himself. He wrote later that:

> The [*Kaiserschlacht*] battle cost me a great deal also. [Our] youngest son fell on the 23rd of March. He was a flying officer, and was at first reported missing. Then on the battlefield we found a grave with the English inscription: 'Here rest two German flying officers.' I had the sad task of identifying my son. Now he rests in German soil, [but] the war has spared me nothing.

Cheerful Sacrifice?

Although the Michael offensive had forced huge gaps in the British Fifth Army Line and advanced up to 40 miles in places, it was at great cost and for little, if any, strategic advantage. The British General Sir Hubert Gough had been a most prominent casualty when relieved of his command, but his battered divisions had not broken. Within a week, Ludendorff had lost in excess of 250,000 men in an offensive that had promised so much on the first day, but was doomed once it became clear that the British refused to crack.

85

The German Offensives of 1918

British casualties in the same period were 178,000, but almost half were prisoners of war, and the French had lost around 77,000. But the German casualties were excessively high amongst the stormtroops and specially trained infantry of the attack divisions. The losses would be unsustainable if the rate continued.

Losses were one thing, but failure to crack the British defences had led to a fateful downturn in morale. On 30 March, attacks on the left flank by Second Army were as ineffective as those during the abortive Operation Mars. One regiment of the German 18th Division involved on the 30th recorded:

> There was little time for preparation, poor artillery support and the English machine guns were so well hidden that they could not be knocked out. [Overall] the power of the attack was exhausted. Spirits sank to zero. The division suffered a reverse the like of which it had not yet experienced.

By now, the soldiers' mothers, sisters, wives and lovers on the Home Front were no longer in the dark about the scale of the disappointment. It was clear that the promised breakthrough had not materialized after the promise of swift success – and that the German advance that had occurred had been achieved at enormous cost once more. Those witnessing the return of casualties and the departure of more battalions from across the country began to fear that another indecisive and interminably bloody year was about to unfold again.

4–5 April: Villers-Bretonneux – A Desperate Drive Towards Amiens

Ludendorff needed to consolidate and maximise the strength that remained. But logic and cool thinking were not qualities that he had in abundance after the failure of Operation Michael. Despite fixing on another major offensive in the Lys/Flanders sector to the north, as March turned into April, he attempted to revive the offensive on the Somme by seizing Amiens.

Officially, Ludendorff sought to exploit his southern flank and sweep into Amiens before the British or French could consolidate their defences in front of the city. Seventh, Eighteenth and Seventeenth

Casualties

Armies would hold onto their guns and stand fast until Second Army had pushed on to Amiens.

Second Army's attempt failed: its leading assault wave, including 9th Bavarian Reserve and Guards Ersatz Division, were blocked and then driven back in front of Villers-Bretonneux, some 10 miles short of Amiens, by the Australian 9th Brigade and British 14th and 18th Divisions. German accounts reported that: 'The Bavarian Division was forced to withdraw in the face of strong counter-attacks [...] [and] the Guards Ersatz Division, on its left, had reached Cachy (just south of Villers-Bretonneux), but also lost the ground that it had gained that afternoon.'

Crown Prince Rupprecht noted on the evening of 5th April: 'Orders were issued on the evening of the 4th [of April] to continue the attack on the 5th, but it was then discovered that the Allies had offered 'a particularly obstinate resistance' [...] and it was no longer possible to throw the enemy back ...'

German operations on 5 April led the Kaiser's Generals to ponder on another costly disappointment. Crown Prince Rupprecht was forced to concede that: 'The final result of the day is the unpleasant fact that our offensive has come to a complete stop, and its continuation without careful preparation promises no success.'

Casualties

The British Official History, which made a painstaking compilation of casualty statistics, quotes a total of 177,739 men lost as killed, wounded and missing. Of these, almost 15,000 died. Of the 90,000 missing, a large number were taken prisoner as the Germans advanced.

The greatest losses were to 36th (Ulster) Division (7,310), 16th (Irish) Division (7,149) and 66th (2nd East Lancashire) Division (7,023). All three formations were effectively destroyed and had to be taken out of the order of battle to be rebuilt. Six other divisions each lost more than 5,000 men.

By comparison, German casualties overall for the period of both the Somme and subsequent Lys offensives were given as 348,300. As was most graphically demonstrated on the disastrous day of Operation Mars (28 March) a higher proportion of German assault divisions lost in excess of 50 per cent casualties in single actions and most had the heart of their units, namely the remaining experienced and well-drilled officers and NCOs, ripped out of them either in action or by the ever more desperate higher command's attempt to fill the gaps in the stormtroop ranks. It is not surprising, then, that almost one-third of the total German casualties for this period were posted as killed or missing in action.

Ludendorff: Master of Delusion

Ludendorff had admitted by this time that, by the end of 4 April, 'The enemy's resistance was beyond our strength,' and, bizarrely, given the butcher's bill in German casualties, that: 'We must not get drawn into a battle of attrition [as this] would not suit our strategic or tactical situation.'

Rupprecht's Chief of Staff, General Hermann von Kuhl, summed up the opening fortnight of the German spring offensive by stating that:

> Strategic success was illusory with 'Operation Michael' [and Mars] [...] the great tactical success had cost heavy sacrifices, some ninety divisions in all having to be engaged. The conclusion of the fighting left our troops [...] in very unfavourable positions, which led to extraordinary wastage.

In the face of the reality, the master delusionist Ludendorff called it a 'brilliant feat', which had cost much of the cream of his specially trained stormtroops and first-line divisions. His best card had now been played, but the outcome was not a breakthrough but a bloody draw. Somehow, Ludendorff, Hindenburg and the German General Staff would have to find a way to make good their apparent misfortune in this high stakes game. It was an ironic 'triumph' of ill-informed ambition over reality, which was to be characteristic of the offensives to follow.

Meanwhile, the next throw of the dice was for a sector where, perhaps, the *Kaiserschlacht* should have been launched in the first place: Flanders.

April–July: *Friedenssturm*

April–July: *Friedenssturm* – Ludendorff's Strategic Inconsistencies Exposed

'We are not retreating. We are merely advancing to the rear.'

(Anon)

With the bloody débâcle of Operation Mars, *Kaiserschlacht* was effectively finished in the Somme and Scarpe sectors. In spite of this catastrophe, Ludendorff was still convinced that the British must remain the main target. He hurriedly prepared to mount yet another offensive, this time in the area of the River Lys and around Ypres in the north of the British sector. Ludendorff's sense of humour was still intact, for the March offensive that had seen the failure of the main element of *Kaiserschlacht* now had an overarching name for the following offensives, *Friedenssturm* – the 'Peace Offensive'. *Friedenssturm* would lead to peace: but not quite the way Ludendorff had planned.

9–29 April: Operation Georgette

Preceded by Operation Archangel as a diversionary attack in the French Aisne sector on 6 April, Operation Georgette was to take place in Flanders and aimed to capture the vital railhead at Hazebrouck, in order to cut off the BEF from its supply routes and rear areas as far as the coast. The operation was renamed Georgette rather than George, its original code name: plans had to be scaled down, as the German losses in March had been so heavy. Georgette was to be launched on 9 April, Ludendorff's fifty-third birthday.

The German Sixth Army, under General Ferdinand von Quast, was ordered to attack between Armentières and Givenchy, tear the British defences apart and advance north-west to the important road and rail junction at Hazebrouck. On 10 April, General Sixt von Armin's Fourth Army was to assault the Ypres salient sector and wrest the Messines Ridge from British hands. Sixt von Armin was determined to pinch out the 'salient' where his Fourth Army had suffered so badly during the Messines and Third Ypres/Passchendaele campaign the previous year.

The German Offensives of 1918

The German plan appeared sound, but the British defences were stronger here than had been the case on 21 March and not surprisingly many of the German divisions were inferior to those used in Operation Michael. Fifty per cent of the assault units tasked for Georgette were hastily trained, but second echelon 'trench' as opposed to 'attack' divisions. The one German advantage was that the BEF in this sector was desperately short of reserves to plug any gaps that may be forced in the British line.

Von Quast had eight attack divisions in the first assault wave and six in the second against four British divisions, 34th, 40th, 2nd Portuguese and 55th from north to south, defending the sector between Armentières and Béthune. None of the fourteen German divisions had taken part in the March offensives and were brought into action after retraining for the assault from a period out of the line at rest. The 43rd Reserve Division, which faced 55th Division in the south of the attack sector, had come from Russia.

The offensive was mounted on 9 April, as planned, and opened with the typical hurricane bombardment. A familiar pattern soon emerged. As with Operation Michael, the attack was made through thick fog and, with the damage and further obscuration caused by the massive bombardment, the German offensive began with some excellent progress, which included brushing the dispirited 2nd Portuguese Division aside and advancing up to 3½ miles towards Hazebrouck by the end of the first day. The 1st Bavarian Reserve Regiment of 1st Bavarian Reserve Division, attacking in the Portuguese sector, recorded in its war diary that: 'The trench garrisons surrendered after only feeble resistance.' The 141st Regiment of 35th Division reported: 'First system taken without resistance. In the second our first prisoners were taken. 9.45 a.m., stiff resistance at strongpoint V which was captured and 70 Portuguese taken [prisoner].'

The German 42nd Division, assaulting the line on the left flank of the Portuguese defence and right-hand units of the British 40th Division, broke through all the hostile positions and cut an uninterrupted swathe to Estaires and Bac St Maur on the River Lys. By the afternoon, the leading units were across the river and preparing to advance still further. Its progress, and that of the 1st and 8th Bavarian

Reserve Divisions to its left, depended on equal success by the German attacks to their south.

Spoiling Ludendorff's Birthday

The hapless Portuguese were unwittingly providing Ludendorff with an early birthday present, but elsewhere the promise of breakthrough was left cruelly unfulfilled. As the German 42nd Division swept all before it, the German assault was about to be stopped in its tracks by the bloody-minded determination of one British division near Givenchy.

The English 55th Division was deployed on the extreme right of the British sector facing the German onslaught, its troops dug in and up against the German IV Korps, with three divisions, the 18th Reserve, 43rd Reserve and 4th Ersatz Divisions, in the leading assault waves. The divisions attacked under the impression that they were facing a 'tired British division [...] only fit for holding a quiet sector of the line.' They were soon put to rights. The 55th Division was fully prepared to meet any attack and, in stark contrast to their Portuguese neighbours, every man was aware of his responsibilities in resisting the German thrust. As the battle developed to their left, the men of 55th Division formed a defensive flank to shore up their own defences against a German breakthrough from the Portuguese sector.

At 0900 hours, large groups of assault troops from 18th Reserve Division appeared close to the newly established defensive flank on 55th Division's left. As soon as they could be seen plainly through the mist, the advancing Germans were cut down and the survivors driven back to seek shelter in the former Portuguese positions. When the main German attack against 55th Division was launched at 0845 hours, the German troops were well protected by the fog and a most effective creeping barrage.

The leading assault wave was on top of the forward defences before the British defenders could react. But once the barrage lifted, the momentum of the attack was lost almost immediately as the groups that had penetrated the British defences were killed or captured and the following waves were chopped up by machine-gun, rifle, artillery and mortar fire. Despite this setback, the attackers of 43rd Reserve and 4th Ersatz Divisions were determined to break the back of 55th

The German Offensives of 1918

Division's defence. By 10 a.m., they had worked their way forward to Givenchy church and were close to the canal on the Cuinchy road. They appeared to be on the threshold of success, but the pendulum swung once again over the next two hours as the British strongpoints held out and counter-attacks drove back the desperate German efforts to hold on to their gains.

By midday the British defenders had largely restored the situation. Further attacks continued in the afternoon and some German troops managed to infiltrate beyond the main defences and close in on field artillery in action, only to be killed or driven back by the guns firing point-blank at them.

The German assaults were beaten back time after time, and when the fog began to clear, the unfolding disaster against 55th Division became apparent as the wire in front of their defences was seen festooned with dead and dying German troops. The final act came with the capture of no less than 640 Germans trapped within the network of British barbed wire and left with no choice but to surrender. Two German battalion commanders and their tactical staff groups, over 100 machine guns and automatic rifles and over 620 officers and men, including a band with its instruments, were taken.

This motley crew of German troops and two COs from battalions of the 4th Ersatz Division was the last 'main event' within 55th Division's area. Operation Georgette had mixed results by the end of its first day, but in the south, it had been stopped in its tracks by a well trained, disciplined and stubborn defence. German accounts acknowledged their failure against 55th Division, although not always accurately. Rupprecht noted on the evening of 9 April: 'In Givenchy, the 55th Division, a particularly good Scottish [sic] division, offered obstinate resistance.'

The last word on this day and this German 'difficulty' had to go to Ludendorff himself, who wrote that:

In the evening [in the north] we were advancing towards Armentières, had reached the Lys and we were approaching the Lawe. In the direction of Béthune we made little progress. On the left, at Givenchy and Festubert, we were held up. The result was not satisfactory.

92

10 April: A Better Day

The 55th Division had spoiled Ludendorff's birthday as surely as it had been spoiled in 1917 on the opening day of the British Arras offensive.

10 April: A Better Day but the British Bulldog Will Not Lie Down

On the 10th, General Sixt von Armin's Fourth Army launched its assault against the blood-soaked Messines Ridge, where the British had blown the formerly 'impregnable' German defences of Wytschaete Bogen apart in June the previous year. It was defended by IX British Corps, and Messines by 25th Division, which had taken part in the British offensive here in 1917. The Fourth Army attacked with two Korps, XVIII Reserve in the north and X Reserve in the south, each with two divisions in the first assault waves.

The preliminary bombardment began at 0245 hours and the main assault was launched promptly at 0515 hours through thick mist and across previously laid pontoon bridges across the Lys. 17th Reserve Division, of XVIII Korps, captured Messines and then some of the ridge as they advanced beyond the village, but the leading battalions were rapidly stopped near Wulverghem by stiff British resistance and then counter-attacks. Units of 49th Reserve Division (of Fourth Army reserve) were sent in to support 17th Reserve Division and held a defensive line against the British countermoves between Hill 63 and the southern end of Messines across the Douve valley for the rest of the day.

To their south, X Korps had attacked with 31st and 214th Divisions in the van and pushed forward to take Ploegsteert Wood, Ploegsteert village and the northern part of the Armentières sector. Parties of German assault troops from 31st Division infiltrated through the forward British positions in Ploegsteert Wood, but a rock-solid defence soon repulsed the main attacks. The 214th Division captured Ploegsteert village and then resolutely held on to its gains despite several fierce British counter-attacks.

General von Quast's Sixth Army resumed its attacks after 9 April at 0600 hours on the 10th. North to south, II Bavarian Korps, XIX and LV Korps pushed on between Nieppe/Steenwerck and Givenchy/Festubert after regrouping and replenishment overnight. All along the front, the Sixth Army advance was stalled by determined counter-attacks and losses mounted drastically. Both OHL and Rupprecht's Group of Armies HQ made every effort to rush in reinforcements, mainly from Seventeenth Army, to press home the attacks. With these new units expected overnight, orders were issued to Sixth Army on the evening of 10 April to take the high ground around Meteren and Bailleul on the Franco-Belgian border and to capture the crossings over the La Bassée canal on the following day.

11 April: 'Backs to the Wall'

Ludendorff was heartened by the German efforts on 10 April when he was informed that the British had abandoned Armentières, which lay between the converging attacks of Sixt von Armin's Fourth and von Quast's Sixth Armies. Although British resistance had already been fierce and a number of Operation Georgette's aims had been frustrated, Ludendorff still believed that the 'English' would crack under the continued pressure. He would have been greatly encouraged by Field Marshal Haig's appeals for French assistance in the face of the German onslaught, which appeared to go unheeded.

The fact remained that by early on 11 April, the forward units of Sixth Army were less than 5 miles from the vital town of Hazebrouck and both British and French chiefs had every reason to be most concerned about the implications of its loss. On 11 April, Field Marshal Haig issued a special order of the day in which he emphasized that:

> There is no other course open to us but to fight it out. Every position must be held to the last man: there must be no retirement. With our backs to the wall and believing in the justice of our cause each one of us must fight on to the end.

Haig's stirring appeal was of little use to the troops fighting on that day, but it did later add further steel to the resolve of the British and Dominion troops fighting tooth and nail to prevent a German breakthrough. The 11th was a significant day, for the British defences were bolstered by the arrival of the British 5th, 33rd and the 1st Australian Divisions, just as the momentum of Georgette began to ebb and agreement was reached between Haig and Marshal Ferdinand

11 April: 'Backs to the Wall'

Foch on French support at this crucial time. By the 14th, Foch had been elevated to Generalissimo of the Allied Armies and introduced a roulement of fresh and battle weary divisions, so that by the 19th, French infantry had taken over a 9-mile stretch in the centre of the British Second Army's sector in Flanders.

On the other hand, Ludendorff had already lost that luxury and, as with Operation Michael, his troops were becoming exhausted and heartily disillusioned. He decided to appeal to their honour and courage one more time by promising the prize of Ypres and the pinching out of the 'salient' in which so many thousands of German soldiers had been lost alongside the British, French, Dominion and Belgian dead since 1914. But they were frustrated once again when the British reluctantly – though wisely – withdrew from Passchendaele to a tighter defensive perimeter around Ypres and smashed all German assaults against the town.

Home Front attitudes were now changing and the role of the BEF in holding on against the best that the German war machine could throw against them was earning a grudging, though honest respect at the highest levels. The following quote comes from the pen of Evelyn, Princess Blücher:

> The so-called victories have been painted in glowing colours [...] and morally, too, the offensives carried out so far have not made the wished-for impression on the enemy [to undermine their morale], but if anything the attacks have put new courage into them [...] We hear universally that the pluck shown by the English [*sic*] (i.e. British and Dominion troops) was almost superhuman [...] Even Ludendorff, hard stern man that he is, confessed that he would take off his hat to the English for their absolutely undaunted bravery. It is reported that he said that they never lose their heads and never appear desperate; they are always cool and courageous until the very moment of death or capture.

By the final week in April, Operation Georgette was looking perilously close to failure and Ludendorff's frustrations were manifest. He was still obsessed by his desire to beat the British, but once again,

Fatal Interlude: The Death of the Red Baron

Whilst the ebb and flow of the Lys offensive reached the final stages, the Somme provided the headlines on 21 April. Baron Manfred von Richthofen, Germany's greatest ace, knight of the air and commander of the famous 'Flying Circus', was finally shot down and fatally wounded.

His death sent shock waves through the German Army and air arm alike, for he was a great inspiration to those serving at the front and to the German people. Although he had been wounded previously, his fellow pilots and the soldiers on the ground imagined him immortal, and he was a true hero of the Fatherland.

The manner of his death was controversial, as his 'kill' was claimed by Captain Albert Brown of 209 Squadron RAF and Australian Lewis machine-gunners. The ground fire was most probably von Richthofen's *coup de grâce*, and when his body was recovered he was buried with full military honours at Bertangles British military cemetery, accompanied by an Australian Honour Guard.

they had proved they could tough it out against his best efforts to dislodge or destroy them. Now the French were making their mark in support of their ally, as his forces were becoming exhausted and severely depleted. However, he had one or two more cards up his sleeve: the time had come to play them.

24–25 April: The Somme and 'Villers-Bret'

A frustrated Ludendorff renewed his efforts in the south. By 24 April his troops had reached the village of Villers-Bretonneux ('Villers-Bret' to its British and Australian defenders), less than 10 miles from Amiens. Villers-Bret had been the scene of a failed assault on 4 and 5 April, immediately before Georgette.

The German attack on Villers-Bretonneux included the very first tank versus tank engagement in the history of warfare, featuring British Mk IV tanks and one of the few German A7Vs. The A7V had a crew of eighteen, was armed with one 57-millimetre gun and six machine guns. It had a top speed of a mere 3 miles per hour. In comparison, the ubiquitous British Mk IV had a similar speed, a crew of eight, and came in two versions: the 'male', armed with two 6-pounder naval guns and two machine guns, and the 'female', armed with just four machine guns.

On the edge of the wood of Bois l'Abbe, 1½ miles south-west of Villers-Bretonneux, was a section of British Mk IV tanks, a 'male' and two 'females', which were deployed to support the dug-in infantry. Suddenly an A7V lurched into view and the British tanks moved forward to engage it.

The British section commander, Lieutenant Frank Mitchell, in the 'male' Mk IV, fired at the German A7V, but missed and the German tank kept on coming. The A7V then halted and opened fire, hitting both 'female' tanks, which were forced to withdraw. But Mitchell's tank continued to advance. After a brief but hot exchange of fire the A7V was hit and the damaged German monster then withdrew.

The abortive tank attacks were part of Ludendorff's increasingly desperate attempt to find a way through the British defences. As battle raged in Flanders, German resources had been diverted for another thrust towards Amiens. German assault units occupied much of Villers-Bretonneux by 24 April. If Ludendorff could seize and hold the village, which was astride the ramrod-straight St Quentin to Amiens road, then his logistical problems might be alleviated in this crucial area and his troops resupplied, reinvigorated and ready to make the final thrust towards Amiens itself.

Knowing the stakes were that high, an Allied counter-attack was rapidly organized. Aided by the British 18th (Eastern) Division, the Australian 15th Brigade, led by Brigadier 'Pompey' Elliot attacked to the north of the village and Brigadier Glasgow's 13th Brigade attacked to the south. Both brigades met at the eastern edge of Villers-Bret and the Germans occupying it were effectively surrounded. The final counter-attack was launched on the night of 24/25 April and it was carried through with extraordinary skill (as a night assault is difficult enough even today with all the night-vision aids available) and extreme ferocity. Few German prisoners were taken, and by dawn on the 25th, the surviving defenders, knowing their cause to be an utterly hopeless one, surrendered willingly. The Aussie/British counter-attack was a complete success. 'Villers-Bret' and Amiens were saved and remained in Allied hands for the rest of the war.

The German Offensives of 1918

25–29 April: Flanders and the Final Days of Georgette

Back in Flanders, the final bloody days of Operation Georgette were played out and yet again, the German effort came to nought, for the main objective of Hazebrouck lay out of reach.

But there was one more 'sweet' success for the German High Command to enjoy. After almost four years of Allied occupation, the dominating feature of Mount Kemmel, or Kemmelberg, was captured by the élite German Alpine Corps on 25 April from a French garrison that had only just taken over after spirited British resistance. The Kaiser noted with satisfaction that Mount Kemmel had been taken according to plan. Yet more champagne was consumed: this time to 'The Kemmel heroes'. It was the last cause for celebration during Operation Georgette.

The final effort came four days later, when seven divisions of the Fourth Army attacked on a ten-mile front from Ypres to the River Douve. Foch had brought the strength of the French-held sector up to seven divisions as well as providing strong artillery reserves. This time, except for two small penetrations, the Allied line held. With his Fourth and Sixth Armies so exhausted as to be extremely vulnerable to counter-attack, Ludendorff broke off the offensive.

The brunt of the battle so far had been borne by Haig's hard-pressed troops. As a result of the almost continuous fighting since 21 March, just forty-eight of the sixty-one British divisions in France (two had recently arrived from Palestine) were fit for battle. Eight had been reduced to mere cadres of survivors and in some cases, the divisions would not be fully reconstituted. On the other hand, French C-in-C Pétain's forces were in better condition. At the beginning of May, the French still had 103 divisions, most reinforced to full strength, with sixty-three in the line, including four in Flanders, and forty in reserve. Pétain had an additional two Italian divisions, which had arrived in the latter part of April, alongside three American divisions.

The number of German divisions on the Western Front had been increased to 204 by further arrivals from Russia, although Ludendorff was very worried about the lack of drafts to replace his losses. The lack of quality manpower was now one of his greatest concerns. Shifting the blame for this entirely on others' shoulders, he angrily complained about the Government's failure to release exempted men and take 'energetic action against deserters and shirkers'.

29 April: The BEF Remains Undefeated and Standing Firm

The twenty-ninth of April 1918 was a crucial date, for it was then that Ludendorff tacitly acknowledged that he had failed to achieve his principal aim: to destroy the British Army in France and Belgium. Legends, half-truths and myths have grown out of the German attempts to crush the BEF before knocking France out of the war, not least of which is the false observation that the main aim was to split the British and French armies, rather than seek principally to annihilate the BEF's fighting capability.

Ludendorff had made fundamental mistakes, not least of which was to suggest that his strategy would take care of itself as long as his tactics were sound. Though successful to a degree, stormtroop tactics were largely self-defeating once the British learned to deal with the increasingly predictable German infiltration methods and the subsequent main advance by the attack divisions.

Ludendorff had failed to learn another critically important lesson from his predecessor. In 1916 von Falkenhayn concluded not only that the Western Front was the main theatre of the war, but also that Britain was the arch-enemy and the 'soul' of Allied resistance against the Central Powers. Most importantly, he was already certain that the German Army was not strong enough to defeat the British and force their withdrawal to the Channel ports while simultaneously pinning the French south of the River Somme. This was a major reason for Falkenhayn's decision to attack the French at Verdun rather than the British in another sector of the Western Front in early 1916. The events of 1916 bore out Falkenhayn's views, for the British Army proved a formidable counter to the German Army, after a bad start, on the Somme.

With the exception of Liège in August 1914, Ludendorff's experience of the offensive and open warfare had come only from the Eastern Front. However, with the temporary advantage of transferring a million men from that theatre of war in early 1918, he decided to ignore the lessons of 1916 and 1917 and was conceited enough to

The German Offensives of 1918

believe that he could destroy the British Army in place and that French capitulation would follow like night follows day. The success of *Kaiserschlacht* hinged on surprise and overwhelming penetration of the British sector on a limited front, in order to tear the defences apart and trigger paralysis of command and resistance on the part of the British. It was a pipe dream, and like the Schlieffen Plan in 1914, it took little account of the quality of the enemy facing the German onslaught.

When the Somme and Lys offensives failed, some German commanders in the field and influencers back home lay the blame at the feet of the troops. This was later encapsulated in an article that asked why the great spring offensive had petered out after a few days, after showing so much promise at the outset. It suggested that:

> The key to the riddle must be sought principally in the psychological and physical condition of the troops. The best of the old German Army lay dead on the battlefields of Verdun and the Somme [...] As time passed, the picture gradually changed for the worse [...] the number of peacetime officers in a unit grew smaller and [...] they were replaced by young fellows of the very best will, but often without sufficient knowledge. At the same time, the old corps of NCOs rapidly disappeared, so that finally the difference between NCO and private soldier vanished, very much to the detriment of discipline.

This analysis does not ring true, for if the loss of experienced officers and NCOs was the only criterion for an army's failure, the British and French would have been fatally weakened as well. The root of the problem was not so much the German soldier as the tactics imposed and leadership at the highest level.

The fundamental responsibility for the failure of Michael, Mars and Georgette was the impossible mission given to the German troops by Ludendorff. His original plan was, like the Schlieffen Plan, too ambitious, and took too little account of the enemy's capabilities. Ludendorff, a 'chancer' who believed that strategy would fall naturally out of successful tactics, seemed to choose the most unimaginative and

29 April: The BEF Remains Undefeated and Standing Firm

dogmatic approaches to his stated aim of breaking through British lines and then destroying the BEF. Rather than seeking the weakest points of the British sector, he launched attacks against Arras (Mars) and Ypres (Georgette), which met fierce, well-organized and highly effective defences and cost the German assault troops dear. Though battered, the British were unbowed and had emerged from the opening German offensives confident that they could match the best that the German Army could offer.

After Georgette there was an inevitable lull as both Ludendorff and the Allied commanders took stock. By the end of April, the German offensives against the British sector on the Somme, around Arras and in Flanders, had resulted in almost 350,000 casualties. The BEF had taken 240,000 casualties, of which around half had become POWs, and the French 92,000 killed, missing, wounded and POWs. But the 'parity' between enemies hid the fact that the Germans had lost most of their first line stormtroops and specially trained attack division personnel. They were irreplaceable: their slaughter and the failure of the breakthrough tactics against the increasingly stubborn British and Dominion forces left Ludendorff on the horns of a dilemma. Worse, the German manpower crisis was hardly matched by a similar prospect for the Allies: the Americans were coming, and they would soon be coming in an ever-rising tide. By 1 May 1918, the American Expeditionary Force (AEF) had 430,000 men in France and US divisions were around 28,000 strong – almost twice the establishment of British, French or German divisions at this stage of the war. By the end of May, the US total rose to 650,000 men.

Coupled with this unpalatable fact, Ludendorff recognized that over the past weeks of the offensive there was a significant contrast between the dogged British spirit in adversity and the rapidly deteriorating quality and discipline of his assault troops. The failure of Michael and Mars had lowered general morale and led to some divisions attacking only after some serious coercion during Operation Georgette. The widespread examples of looting and drunkenness amongst the units that captured British supply dumps and houses in French villages with well-stocked wine cellars during Operation Michael underlined the problem of morale. These breaches of the 'Prussian tradition' to carry out orders without question, and the legacy of the huge casualty bill since 21 March were worrying signs, and serious concerns were put to Ludendorff by his commanders and staffs. Crown Prince Rupprecht and General Fritz von Lossberg, Chief of Staff of Fourth Army, stated that there might be little value in persisting with further offensives, and although Ludendorff disagreed, he did concede that dwindling manpower and *matériel* made it impossible to carry out two simultaneous large-scale offensives. Delay between one offensive and another was not only logical but also crucial to allow time for the redeployment of the 'battering train' and concentration of the forces required.

With these considerations in mind, Ludendorff fixed his attention next to a hastily conceived 'Plan B' for defeating the BEF on the Flanders plain. He aimed to draw the French south in a series of smaller-scale attacks and separate them from the BEF. His view was that the British would be isolated and vulnerable, with their backs to the sea, as well as the wall. Therefore, the German offensives would now turn on the French

L'Affaire Française: The First Three Weeks in May

During the lull in the German offensives in May, German, British and French troops manned the line as they had done for years across the Western Front and slipped back into more routine defensive ways, which were interrupted at times by the odd trench raid from both sides and exchanges of artillery fire. Typical of this daily life on both sides of the wire at this time was that contained in a letter from a captured German soldier who was facing the Australian 7th Infantry Brigade of 2nd Australian Division and British troops near Hamel in the Amiens sector:

Morlancourt, 5th May 1918

Dearest Mother,

Have received your letter and was delighted to receive news from my dear and distant home. Write to me often, even if I do not write to you often, as I rarely get the chance, though whenever I do I will always write. We are here near Albert town [and] I am on the foremost line, about 200 metres opposite the British. We have Australians here and they are very cunning. They creep up in the night like cats to our trenches so that we don't notice them. Last night they were in our trench, killed two men and dragged one away with them. I am glad that we are so far forward as we at least get very little artillery fire here. Our regiment has already had heavy casualties from gas – that is one of the most terrible deaths one can suffer, to swallow gas. I am very careful about it and always have my gas mask with me. There are a lot of new soldiers here, but I haven't met anyone I know. They are mostly Bavarians, Badeners and Rheinlanders. The worst of all here are the [English] airmen. We hardly dare move for fear of them. Please God that I may come out safe. We are to be relieved on Whitsunday. Is there any news from home?

Goodbye [for now],

Your,

Otto.

Ludendorff's Logic for the Next Big Idea

A number of senior officers, including Crown Prince Rupprecht of Bavaria, General von Lossberg and General von Kuhl, were already dubious about the value of further offensives after the failure of Operations Michael, Mars and Georgette.

For his part, Erich Ludendorff did at least acknowledge that it was no longer possible to sustain two major offensives at the same time and that delays between offensives were inevitable and necessary, reflecting the need for regrouping, reinforcement, redeployment to the chosen sector for the attack, further training, orders and rehearsals. In short, the German 'battering train' had to be moved and this had to take time. But Ludendorff knew that the transient numerical German advantage was a rapidly dwindling asset. Therefore, more assaults were vital if the Fatherland was to witness the great victory promised before the scales tipped decisively in favour of the Allies instead.

The German Offensives of 1918

Ludendorff's principal objective was still to beat the British, and in Flanders, although at the beginning of May, he judged that he must first force French reserves towards the south, which would leave Haig without a strategic reserve when the time came for the main event in Flanders. So, he decided to attack the weaker French defences in the Chemin des Dames sector in Champagne, commanded by General Denis Auguste Duchêne.

27 May–6 June: Operation Blücher-Yorck

Operation Blücher-Yorck was launched against the Chemin des Dames, where the French Nivelle offensive had come to grief almost a year before. With a month's gap between Georgette and Blücher, OHL had studied and applied many of the lessons learned from Michael, Mars and Georgette. The key was revision of the artillery's role, especially in the effectiveness of the creeping barrage to protect the assaulting infantry. Infiltration tactics made it very difficult to apply flexible fire plans, so one practical change was to allocate an artillery battery to each infantry regiment, making it 'under command' and committed to providing timely indirect fire for that regiment. Much effort had gone into specialist training for fresh troops, which were incorporated into the assault divisions, and stormtroop tactics were modified for the different terrain and French defensive layout.

General von Boehn's Seventh Army faced the French Sixth Army under General Duchêne, augmented by five divisions of the British IX Corps, sent to this sector to recuperate after fighting in both the March and April offensives. With the evil irony that besets some in war, three of the divisions of IX Corps were in the front line when the offensive crashed into the forward positions on 27 May.

Ludendorff's choice of the Chemin des Dames was sound, for the layout of the French defences here invited catastrophe. General Duchêne committed the cardinal sin of packing his forward positions with troops, although the Allied doctrine had changed to that of flexible or elastic defensive tactics. Duchêne had failed to appreciate that if the German attack was preceded by a heavy artillery bombardment, which it was, his front-line units would be smashed before the assaulting German infantry went over the top.

27 May–6 June: Operation Blücher-Yorck

On the other side, von Boehn had the advantage of being given all the assistance for Operation Blücher-Yorck that had been noticeably absent during the April offensive in Flanders. Therefore, Seventh Army's assault divisions had the benefit of a preliminary 160-minute hurricane bombardment of 4,000 guns: another classic orchestration by Colonel Georg Bruchmüller. The German barrage began at 0100 hours on 27 May and 'was of a violence and accuracy that in the opinion of the most seasoned soldiers far outdid any other barrage that they had experienced'.

The concentration of fire was even greater than that on 21 March and the initial bombardment was a mix of gas and high explosive (HE) at maximum rate of fire. The next phase targeted front-line trenches and belts of barbed wire alongside counter-battery (CB) work and then rear area targets such as railheads, troop billets and HQ/communication centres were hit with heavy and medium barrages. Finally, the French and British defenders were rocked by drumfire from virtually all the guns as Zero Hour approached.

At 3.40 a.m. seventeen German attack divisions, with the storm-troop units in the van and protected by creeping barrages and heavy machine-gun fire, rushed forward to assault the Chemin des Dames. The troops of Duchêne's Sixth Army were taken completely by surprise and then stunned by the violence of the whirlwind artillery bombardment. A Gendarme, attached to the French 47th Division wrote:

Sunday 26th May:

With the 19th at Vaux Varennes [and carried out patrols]. Very calm, absolutely no gunfire.

Monday 27th May:

At 0120 hours shellfire wakes us up, they are very close. I get up. Shells are falling all around and seem to be getting closer. One falls in a garden next our billet, we don't feel very safe. At three o'clock we smell gas. We receive the order to go around and warn the people to have their masks ready. Around six o'clock the bombardment seems to slacken off. It starts again, but even more than before. We don't know what's going on. At 11, a Captain comes but he too knows nothing, seems to think that the attack has failed. It's raining shells and groups of planes pass overhead. Around one o'clock the first evacuees arrive, rumours abound but there is no concrete news. Some say that they [the Germans] have crossed the Aisne and that Roncy has fallen. Boche aeroplanes come over and machine-gun the roads. We still don't know what's happening. Delville goes to Corps HQ at 2 p.m. and comes back an hour later without orders. No one knows what to do and we wait for orders to leave. A group of artillery men arrive saying that all their guns are lost. We realize that things are bad. At 1600 hours we tell people to leave although they can stay if they want to. Two thirds leave but the others prefer to stay [...] The Montigny to Jonchery road is swept by shellfire. The road is choked with refugees, pushing handcarts, horsedrawn carts and so on. What a sad spectacle. There are at least thirty people in the barn where we sleep. The village is full.

From a British perspective, the 8th Division's official history provides graphic detail of the experience of the British IX Corps caught up in the German thrust:

26th May (Evening)

Silence [...] Not a shell came from the enemy, and his quietness removed any lingering doubts as to his intentions.

How that evening dragged. The time crept slowly on towards zero hour till only a few minutes were left ...

27th May (Early a.m.)

Suddenly two German gas shells burst close at hand, punctual heralds of the storm. Within a second, a thousand guns roared out their Iron hurricane. The night was rent with sheets of flame. The earth shuddered under the avalanche of missiles [...] Ever above the din screamed the fierce crescendo of approaching shells, ear-splitting crashes as they burst [...] all the time the dull thud,

27 May–6 June: Operation Blücher-Yorck

thud of detonations [...] the drum fire. Inferno raged and whirled round the Bois des Buttes. The dugouts rocked [...] filled with the acrid fumes of cordite, the sickly sweet tang of gas. Timbers started, earth showered from the roof, men rushed for shelter, seizing kit, weapons, gas masks, message pads as they dived for safety. It was a descent into hell. Crowded with jostling, sweating humanity the dugouts reeked [...] Gas masks were hurriedly donned and anti gas precautions taken. The dugout entrance was closed with saturated blankets, braziers lighted on the stairs. If gas could not enter, neither could air. As a fact both did in small quantities and the long night was spent forty feet underground, at the hottest time of the year, in stinking overcrowded holes, their entrances sealed up and charcoal braziers alight drying up the atmosphere – suffocation rendered more complete by the gas mask with clip on nostrils and gag in teeth.

When the German bombardment erupted at 0100 hours on 27 May the entire IX Corps' front and many rear areas were hit by gas, as well as high explosive shells. The defensive 'Outpost' lines were rocked by trench mortars of every calibre in addition to the artillery barrage. By 0600 hours most of 8th Division's own artillery batteries had been neutralized. A thick mist accentuated by the enemy's gas and smoke shells, grew steadily thicker as dawn approached, making the defenders' task all the more difficult.

The 8th Division's account continues:

The first Infantry attack, assisted by tanks which flattened out the wire, was delivered; it is probable, at about four o'clock in the morning, against the angle of the salient in our right sub-sector (25th Infantry Brigade). Owing to the dense mist and to the fact that nearly all units in the Outpost Zone were cut off to a man, it is difficult to reconstruct precisely the sequence of events. It is only at intervals that a clear message comes back out of the chaos and confusion which the fog necessarily produced. Even such a message only serves to emphasize the assistance which the lack of visibility and the exposed position of our troops in the salient gave to the enemy in his attack. Take for instance, the following pigeon message, the following pigeon, timed at 5.15 a.m., which was received at Divisional Headquarters at 6.05 a.m.: HQ 2nd R. Berks Regt, consisting of Lieutenant Colonel Griffen, Captain Clare, RSM Wokins, Sergt Trinder, Corporal Dobson, Privates Stone, Gregory, Slee, and QM surrounded. Germans threw bombs down dug-outs and pressed on. They appeared to approach from right rear in considerable strength. No idea what has happened elsewhere. Holding out in hopes of relief.

Such hopes were, alas, in vain.

The attack swept forward, and although our troops resisted stubbornly for a time in the Battle Zone and caused severe losses to the enemy on this line, the defence was overwhelmed by weight of numbers. Brigade HQ had been early involved in the fighting, being practically surrounded before it was known that the front line had gone. It was near here that the brigade major, Captain B.C. Pascoe, MC, Rifle Brigade, was killed while making a gallant stand. General Husey and what remained of his HQ Staff fought their way out and moved back to Gernicourt to organize its defences. At 6.30 a.m. General Husey reported to Divisional HQ that he was holding the river line there with the remnants of his brigade. At 7.15 a.m. he further reported that all the bridges east of the junction of the Miette and Aisne had been blown up and that he was holding the high ground west of Gernicourt. Later in the morning General Husey, who had only taken command of the brigade front (vice General Coffin, promoted to Divisional Command) on the 7th May, was badly wounded and gassed, and he died a few days after in German hands.

Meanwhile the fate of the remaining two brigades was being played out. Neither had been seriously attacked until after 0500 hours, but thereafter the German onslaught was relentless. The front-line battalion of the 24th Infantry Brigade (2nd Northamptonshire) was gradually driven back to the Battle Zone. As dawn broke, enemy aircraft flew low over the British lines and strafed the trenches. Lieutenant Colonel Buckle, CO of 2nd Northamptons, whose conduct and example had been an inspiration to his men, was killed outside his

Battalion HQ, but his battalion fought on and in the Battle Zone in this sector the German assault was checked. The 24th Brigade's defensive position was very strong and repeated attacks were beaten off by the 2nd Northamptons and 1st Worcesters.

The last message sent by Colonel Buckle to his front-line companies soon after the German bombardment began:

> All Platoon commanders will remain with their platoons and ensure that the trenches are manned immediately the bombardment lifts. Send short situation wire every half-hour. No short bombardment can possibly cut our wire and if sentries are alert it cannot be cut by hand. If they try it shoot the devils.
>
> C.G. Buckle, Lieutenant Colonel

This message was found pinned on the wall of the battalion HQ dug-out by Colonel Buckle's father, who visited the spot after the Armistice. He found his son's grave close to the entrance, and on each side of the grave a German was buried close to him.

At 0545 hours large numbers of Germans were suddenly observed from the 24th Brigade HQ approaching along the line of the Miette Stream which they had crossed south of the Battle Zone. The main line of defence was taken by this movement in flank and rear and its defenders were cut and surrounded. Major Cartland[12], commanding the 1st Worcestershires, was killed in the trenches with his men and, at 0600 hours, Brigade HQ was itself attacked from the rear. The Staff Captain to the brigade was taken prisoner, and General Haig, and his acting brigade Major (Captain F.C. Wallace, MC) both of whom were suffering from gas, had great difficulty in getting clear. A few others, including the Signals Officer, Intelligence Officer and some of Brigade HQ personnel, managed to fight their way back to La Pecherie Bridge, the defence of which they organized under Captain Pratt, MC, 1st Worcestershire. However, the German assault was pressed home and Captain Pratt's party was cut off.

Meanwhile, 23rd Infantry Brigade was attacked at about the same time as the 24th Brigade and the German onslaught was checked for a short time by the forward battalion, namely 2nd West Yorkshires who were then forced back to the Battle Zone. Here they made their stand alongside 2nd Middlesex and held their ground against all attacks. The 2nd Devonshire maintained their positions in the Bois des Buttes with equal stubbornness. In desperation, the German assault units brought up a number of captured tanks to augment the attacks, but they were rapidly destroyed by French anti-tank guns.

At 0700 hours these battalions were still holding out, but this stubborn defence was already doomed. Both 24th Brigade and 23rd Brigade were outflanked and German infiltration led to a breach between 149th Infantry Brigade of 50th Division on the left flank and 8th Division. As a result of this double thrust the West Yorkshire and Middlesex men were surrounded and cut off.

HQ 23rd Infantry Brigade recorded the events of 27 May as follows:

Dawn began to break, but no news came of any Infantry attack. The Brigade intelligence officer reported that a heavy ground mist rendered observation impossible, but shortly afterwards sent the amazing message: 'Enemy balloons rising from our front line.' Hot upon this message came another from the 24th Brigade: 'Enemy advancing up Miette Stream. Cannot hold out without reinforcements.' Such news was startling in the extreme, but worse was still to come, for at about 5.30 a.m. the 149th Brigade on the left reported: 'Enemy has broken our Battle Line and is advancing on Ville au Bois.' Thus before word had come of the brigade front being assaulted, the enemy had turned both flanks and was advancing on the Bois des Buttes.

The 2nd Devons here were soon in desperate straits. Heavily attacked in front and on both flanks, the battalion slowly fell backwards towards Pontavert. When some distance north of the town, the gallant commanding officer, Lieutenant Colonel R.H. Anderson-Morshead, DSO, refused to retire further and called upon his battalion to take up a position and protect the crossing. This they did, but the enemy coming in from the east along the river finally got into Pontavert itself and the battalion was completely surrounded. However, the 2nd Devons remained at their posts and fought on as if: 'an island in the midst of a sea of a determined enemy, fighting with perfect discipline, and, by the steadiness of their fire, mowing down assault after assault.'[13]

Thus they were in a position in which they were entirely without hope of assistance but fought on grimly. Refusing to surrender and preferring to fight to the last, the battalion was annihilated, its losses comprising the CO, twenty-eight officers and 552 NCOs and men. The battalion was 'cited' in French Army Orders and later awarded the Croix de Guerre. Its self-sacrifice enabled the brigade commander, Brigadier General Grogan, to organize, with the remnants of his brigade, a defensive position on the high ground about la Platrerie, due south of Pontavert and across the river, to which he moved his HQ.

By mid-morning, the remnants of 8th Division were all across the river and the enemy, rapidly following up, was crossing the river also.

The Fate of the Gunners

The German artillery had the British and French battery positions marked and at around 1300 hours a devastating counter-battery barrage began. The British batteries were heavily shelled, at first with gas shells and later with HE, or mixed with HE and gas. HE and gas in mixed doses following the preparatory gas says one battery report, and the enemy shooting seemed uncannily accurate. Under these conditions it was, in many cases, impossible to carry on the counter preparation and harassing fire which was to have continued all night, but it was maintained whenever possible and for as long as possible.

The 5th Battery (XLV Brigade) for instance, continued to fire throughout the night until, at about 0630 hours, German assault troops attacked the battery position. The three guns at the main position of the 57th Battery of the same brigade had been destroyed.

The 8th Divisional Artillery dispositions when the battle opened were as follows: the zone of the 25th Infantry Brigade on the right was covered by the French Group Paul, under Commandant Paul. This group of 75mm guns was deployed south of the Aisne. The 24th Infantry Brigade, in the centre, was covered by the XXXIII Brigade, RFA (Lieutenant Colonel H.G. Fisher, DSO) while the XLV Brigade, RFA (Lieutenant Colonel J.A. Ballard), covered the zone of

111

The German Offensives of 1918

the 23rd Infantry Brigade. Both these brigades of 18-pounder guns were north of the River Aisne. Owing to the circumstances and as a result of the rapid German penetration the brigades were embroiled in hand-to-hand fighting, and guns that had not been destroyed already were ultimately captured by the enemy. As the Artillery Batteries were either surrounded or directly assaulted by determined German troops, breech-blocks were taken out to render the guns useless to the enemy and the men fought on with rifles and Lewis guns. Inevitably, though, virtually all were either killed or captured.

A detailed account has been compiled from survivors' statements of the action of 5th Battery (XLV Brigade) and it appeared to be a typical example of the extraordinary circumstances in which artillerymen found themselves during the German offensives and how so many showed indomitable spirit against the odds. The German counter-battery barrage was sudden and intense, so the men of 5th Battery had to react swiftly. Their actions were recorded:

Gas masks were instantly adjusted and about ten minutes later the rocket sentry reported S.O.S. rockets on the front. The call was immediately responded to by our gunners, Captain J.H. Massey controlling the fire of the battery, while Lieutenant C.E. Large and 2nd Lieutenant C.A. Button commanded their sections. To continue to serve the guns indefinitely during such a terrific bombardment was a physical impossibility for any one man, and Captain Massey, realizing this, organized a system of reliefs, two gunners and one N.C.O. manning each gun. The remainder of the personnel took cover until their turns came round to take their place at the guns [...] After the customary period of fire on the SOS lines, guns were once more laid on counter preparation lines and a steady rate of fire was continued during what seemed an interminable night.

Lieutenant Large and 2nd Lieutenant Button frequently took their places with the gunners in the reliefs, while Captain Massey kept moving from pit to pit and dug-out to dug-out and then to the detached sections, encouraging the detachments and telephonists and reminding them of the splendid traditions of the Royal Regiment [of Artillery] [...] The strain on all concerned was terrific, but at last at about 0645 hours the enemy barrage lifted clear of our position. Instead, however, of the expected respite, large numbers of German infantry and gunners came into view less than 200 yards from the battery position. A few rounds were fired at point-blank range, but it was then reported that Germans were coming up in rear. There was nothing left but to resort to rifles and Lewis guns. Captain Massey, realizing the situation a little earlier, had called for volunteers and pushed off with four gunners and a Lewis gun team to a small mound east of the position to protect the flank. Nothing more was heard of Captain Massey and his men. Lieutenant Large, although wounded in the foot, took the other Lewis gun, 2nd Lieutenant Button, after having destroyed all the maps, papers and records, was last seen moving off with a rifle to assist Captain Massey. The remainder of the battery fought to the last with just their own rifles until they were overwhelmed by sheer weight of numbers.

Only three gunners who were unarmed and were ordered to retire, and one with a rifle who fought his way out, survived. Of the two Forward Observation Officers (FOOs) 2nd Lieutenant C. Counsell and 2nd Lieutenant H. Reakes, and their telephonists, nothing was heard of again.[14]

By 0630 hours the right of the line rested on the Gernicourt position, but between this and the right of the 24th Infantry Brigade there was a gap. The 1st Battalion Sherwood Foresters, which was Divisional Reserve at that time, was ordered to move forward to plug the gap, which it did brilliantly, preventing the enemy crossing the river via La Pecherie Bridge, which was the only practical crossing point for the German assault troops to the Sherwood Foresters' front.

Unfortunately, elsewhere the German onslaught was largely unchecked. The British 23rd Brigade party led by Brigadier General Grogan was outflanked and driven off their makeshift defensive redoubt on the high ground above the village of La Platerie. Once this happened, the remainder of the Brigade's defensive network unravelled and the Sherwood Foresters and the other defenders of the Gernicourt position were ultimately cut off. The great natural strength of the position, which must have made it a most serious obstacle to a direct assault, was of little use when the German assaults were driven home in such force and with such ferocity. The remainder of the Gernicourt garrison, which included a determined French Territorial unit, fought on with tremendous tenacity, but these defenders were inevitably surrounded and by the end of that morning, the garrison ceased to exist. All the guns, i.e. the French 'Soixante Quinzes' and the 18-pounders of VX Brigade RFA, were lost.

The situation was so dire that GOC 8th Division decided soon after 1000 hours to use his remaining reserves – some 600 men from the Lewis Gun School and 'Div troops', such as transport and ordnance soldiers of the Army Service Corps, to hold the second position. This ran along the northern slope of the high ground south of the river Aisne on the general line Bouffignereux–Roucy–Conevreux.

Troops of the 25th Division were already moving up to this line in accordance with IX Corps' orders. At 1320 hours, 75th Infantry Brigade, which had originally been ordered forward from 25th Division to fill a gap between the remnants of the 8th Division and what was left of 50th Division, was put under General Heneker's command. The defensive line was thus held as follows:

On the right, isolated and surrounded, remnants of the 22nd DLI[15] and 1st Sherwood Foresters were still holding parts of the Bois de Gernicourt. The 75th Infantry Brigade was holding the second position from Bouffignereux to Concevreux, with 2nd South Lancashires in the van, alongside the remnants of 24th and 25th Infantry Brigades. On the left, between Roucy and Concevreux, the 11th Cheshires were the most complete unit in the line, boosted by the remaining fighting men of 23rd Infantry Brigade and 8th Border Regiment was in close support behind Roucy. On the divisional right the high ground overlooking the village of Bouffignereux was occupied by the 7th Infantry Brigade and the left flank around Concevreux village was defended by 74th Infantry Brigade/25th Division.

During the afternoon there was a lull in the fighting. Troops who came through the ordeal later noted that by that time, the day was extremely hot, the sunshine brilliant and, but for the deep drone of heavy shells winging their way rearwards, all sounds of battle were temporarily stilled.

The Fate of the Gunners

Viewed from the hills above Roucy the battle area presented a vivid spectacle. The River Aisne and the canal 'glittered like silver ribbons in the sun', while in the vacated trench systems a pall of haze and dust lingered. When it occasionally lifted, there was the eerie, almost surreal sight of the roads in the valley 'field grey thick' with German battalions marching towards their various jumping-off points for further attacks as if they were marching to a grand parade, rather than into battle. Horse-drawn artillery pieces, limbers and wagons clogged up the roads still further.

At this point, Ludendorff's assault troops had the luxury of local air superiority, so they were largely immune from the threat of French aerial attacks. German Observation balloons were brought up very close to the forward lines. British and French soldiers occupying the high ground looked incredulously at the German preparations for fresh attacks developing methodically and without disruption before their very eyes.

As expected, the lull in the fighting for most of the afternoon was brought to an abrupt halt at around 1600 hours. Under cover of a terrific bombardment from artillery, mortars and machine guns, the German assault was renewed all along the line. The British defences on the right were penetrated and the village of Bouffignereux was captured. This success was vigorously exploited and the whole line was soon forced back. By 1915 hours it had been pushed back some 3,000 yards and ran along the tops of the hills separating the valley of the Aisne from the valley of the Vesle. Brigadier General H.A. Kennedy, GOC 75th Infantry Brigade, called urgently for reinforcements and ammunition. The latter was sent at once. To meet the former demand, General Heneker sent out officers to collect all the stragglers they could find and these, supplemented by his HQ guard and the personnel of his HQ – a total force of some 500 men – were sent forward under his ADC, Major G.R. Hennessy and were handed over to General Kennedy at 2200 hours.

Inevitably under such pressure, the defensive line began to buckle and by midnight Ventelay and Bouvancourt were in the hands of the enemy. The German advance was so swift that at one point the entire 25th Divisional Ambulance unit was captured in Bouvancourt. 25th Divisional HQ, which had already fallen back to Montigny-sur-Vesle that afternoon, re-established itself by 2300 hours at Branscourt to the south of the Vesle, but during the night the enemy succeeded in turning the British right flank and once again the remnants of the IX Corps troops in this sector were forced to withdraw to the line of the River Vesle. By dawn on 28 May, Brigadier General Grogan, GOC 23rd Infantry Brigade was ordered to assume command of all troops in the sector centred on the town of Jonchery and to hold a front on the river Vesle extending one mile either side of it.

At the End of the First Day of Operation Blücher-Yorck

Twenty-seventh May was one of extraordinary success for von Boehn and almost unmitigated disaster for Duchêne. The French defences were rolled back to the River Aisne by mid-morning and by the afternoon a huge gap had appeared where the best part of eight French and British divisions had held the line a few hours before. The Aisne bridges behind the forward defence had not been demolished and by evening, the Germans were across the river, had swarmed across the next ridge and reached the River Vesle.

Von Boehn's leading assault units advanced a staggering 10–12 miles by the end of the first day. Compared with the qualified success of the opening day of Operation Michael, Blücher-Yorck was an unequivocal triumph. By the end of the next day, Soissons was in German hands and by 3 June, Ludendorff's leading divisions had reached the Marne – the scene of so much heartbreak for German ambitions in 1914.

Now it seemed that retribution was in the offing, for the Kaiser's men were only 50 or so miles from Paris and their offensive appeared unstoppable once again.

German Gunner Officer Herbert Sulzbach's delight at his part in this historic day and the apparently decisive blow against the French was coloured by other events:

27th May:

Once again, world history has been made, and just as I did on 21 March 1918, beyond St Quentin, I am sitting now in our bivouac in the evening after this splendid victory, but this time with Chavignon behind me: but with a completely different

116

feeling from the mood we were in on 21 March. That time little *Leutnant* Schmidt [...] was sitting beside me on the limber, helping me to make my notes: and now [he] is dead. Only yesterday he was charging about in his battery, as keen, lively and cheerful as ever. He was one of our most daring chaps, and for four weeks he had worn his Iron Cross, First Class, awarded for conspicuous gallantry; but now he is lying in his grave near Monampteuil. Yesterday, before the attack, he was killed, along with a Lance-Sergeant beside him, by a direct hit – and my pleasure at the thought of the offensive left me entirely. Now he is dead, our companion who was always cheerful and eager for hard work. I think now [about how many of my comrades and also former school-friends are no longer there – it is just unbelievable! Apart from this, we had many other losses before the barrage began [against the French positions] [...] at 2 a.m. [*sic*] on 27 May.

As Sulzbach was poignant, rather than elated at the result of the opening day of 'Blücher-Yorck', his Emperor the Kaiser announced that night, after yet another exhausting, but exhilarating visit to the front: 'Gentlemen, a great victory; 10,000 prisoners taken and a host of guns.'

On 31 May, OHL reported that: 'We have reached the Marne and taken Soissons. This evening it was reported that the number of prisoners taken has risen to 45,000 and the number of guns is 400.'

Ludendorff's Certainty Enhanced by Echoes of Victory

Operation Blücher-Yorck's achievement was beyond even Ludendorff's expectations. He was convinced once again that the war was there to be won and decided to reinforce this success, rather than stick with the plan to draw French reserves away from the British sector in the north before then launching his decisive blow in Flanders. Plan 'A' (*Kaiserschlacht*) had become Plan 'B' (Blücher-Yorck and other planned French diversionary attacks to mask a decisive offensive in Flanders) and was now in danger of becoming Plan 'C' (smashing the French Army and marching on Paris). Ludendorff's increasingly ambivalent nature was there for all to see. It was not a pretty sight. Plan 'C' was about to run into a new obstacle – and a new enemy.

The German Offensives of 1918

A New Enemy

Operation Blücher-Yorck raised Ludendorff's hopes, but the momentum of the offensive was stopped around Château Thierry, where the American 2nd and 3rd Divisions supported the French counter-attacks. On 6 June, the 2nd US Division cut the German advance back at Belleau Wood. These were not major actions in the whole scheme of things, but the Germans had been served notice: the Americans were not only coming, but they were spoiling for a fight.

Operation Blücher-Yorck had been a spectacular effort and General von Boehn had achieved a brilliant advance. But, as during Operation Michael in March, the Germans had boxed themselves into a bag: a deep salient. It was a logistic nightmare, as the bulge in the line across damaged roads and rail links made it more and more difficult to resupply and reinforce the troops at the tip of the German thrust into the French guts. A British officer serving in the sector had traced the advance by the changing line of German observation balloons:

> The great sweeping semi-circle in the sky marked out the German position and suggested its dangers in an extraordinarily clear and graphic manner. The possibilities of a counter-offensive, thrusting at either angle of the bulge, was inevitably brought to mind.

Despite the initial hopes of Blücher-Yorck, there was already a feeling that the tide might be turning in the Western Allies' favour. The spirit of the BEF was undiminished, the French had repulsed this latest serious threat and the Americans were on the rise. In Germany, one mother wrote:

> My nephew, just 19 years of age, has just been staying with us. He is on leave after taking his part in the Great Offensive. His descriptions of it are terrible. For some time he was forced to occupy the pitiful trenches, with little to eat apart from what he and his men had found in the English trenches on the first day of his attack [. . .] He described the friendly manner with which they discussed the war with the English officers who were taken prisoner. One Englishman, when asked when peace would come, answered 'Well, I suppose it will take a couple of more years

9–11 June: Operation Gneisenau

before you Germans are really beaten.' Also, he explained that the Americans are daily becoming a more serious asset to the enemy, as each day more troops are pouring in, all fresh and well-equipped in contrast to our tired-out men.

Ludendorff had little choice after 6 June other than to call a halt to Operation Blücher-Yorck. However, in an attempt to expand the salient, consolidate the line and divert more French reserves, he brought in General Oskar von Hutier, the architect of the already legendary 40-mile penetration of the British defences in March, to launch a new offensive.

9–11 June: Operation Gneisenau

The next blow was to fall in the French sector towards the Matz between Montdidier and Noyon on 9 June. Von Hutier's Eighteenth Army assaulted on a 21-mile front against the French Third Army, whose commander, General Humbert, had not quite grasped the in-depth defence methods and made the same mistake of having too many troops forward. Once again, early results looked promising for von Hutier and Ludendorff as the first day ended with an advance of 6 miles, and 8,000 French prisoners. At the Kaiser's Court, Georg Müller noted:

> 9 June. Sunday. The opening of a new offensive on the Montdidier–Noyon Line. The Kaiser left for the front. Spent the whole day at von Hutier's Army HQ seeing nothing but a few clouds of smoke. The offensive is making good progress.

But the momentum slowed more quickly this time than in Operation Blücher-Yorck and the French High Command anticipated and dealt with the, by now, all-too familiar German tactics. On 11 June General Mangin's Tenth Army launched five French divisions, backed by a massive artillery bombardment and low-flying aircraft strafing sorties, carried out the inevitable counter-attack and the German offensive ground to a halt once more. It was a grim result for the German people, as well as the soldiers who had struck so many indecisive blows over the past months. From the predictable high spirits, the German

The German Offensives of 1918

High Command and their Imperial Majesty were struck with equally predictable melancholy:

> News has been received that our right-wing has been halted and counter-attacks have pierced our lines. [Also] from Germany there is news of a terrible drought [...] I felt very depressed [...] The Kaiser was in very low spirits at lunch and ate nothing but a chocolate mousse. Those in the know maintain that the repulse of [the most recent] offensive was the reason.

Counterbalance: The Allies in Early June

Despite French General Mangin's swift riposte and a strong restoration of the Allied line in this sector, Marshal Ferdinand Foch and Philippe Pétain were hardly in a celebratory mood. Foch was visibly shaken by the fall of the Chemin des Dames within a few weeks of his appointment as Allied Generalissimo, as it represented a serious blow to his kudos. Meanwhile, Pétain's melancholy was becoming impossible for the French Staff. The experience of Blücher-Yorck had made French generals less ready to criticize the BEF's performance in March and April.

Blücher-Yorck and Gneisenau: More Nails in the German Coffin

Operation Blücher-Yorck had sorely pressed the Allies, for the amazing success in its first days had put the German Army once more within heavy artillery range of Paris. But the Allies, though battered, bruised and blooded, had come through it all. What's more, they were reinvigorated by the bonus of ever more fit and eager American 'Doughboys' landing on French shores to take the fight to the dogged but largely dispirited German Army on the Western Front. Erich Ludendorff's vision of a decisive breakthrough was now a faded and distant one. By the end of June his problems and shortcomings were multiplying.

Like other German and Allied commanders before him, he had allowed himself to be seduced by early gains and continued each of the offensives for too long, hoping to find the elusive breakthrough. Above all – and unforgivably for a man officially appointed as the

Ludendorff's Certainty Disappears into a Dark Hole

Quartermaster General – he had failed to learn the vital lessons that the railway and motor transport invariably enabled defenders to deploy reserves rapidly to fill gaps in the line and resupply those defending it with ammunition, water, rations and other *matériel* to strengthen the defensive position and the troops' determination to hold on. On the other hand, lack of mobility and the dearth of similar resources to sustain the offensive doomed each one to certain failure once the initial gains had been made. Logistics are a vital factor in the winning and losing of battles, campaigns and wars – and Erich Ludendorff, the Quartermaster General no less, had failed to add such a factor into the equation as part of his recipe for success.

With Blücher-Yorck and Gneisenau now spent, Ludendorff was faced with a bill of over 130,000 further casualties. Once again, the hardest hit were the dwindling number of the youngest, fittest and most able of the junior German officers, SNCOs and men sacrificed in the stormtroop and attack division units. This time, even the extraordinary early gains (and capture of 60,000 Allied prisoners and 850 guns overall) could not soften the blow.

After all, as the British had proved in March and April, guns, ammunition and other lost *matériel* could be swiftly replaced and the Americans were filling the gaps in manpower. On the other hand, Ludendorff's losses in men and *matériel* were desperate, and even he had realized with a heavy heart that it would now be impossible to make good the rapidly haemorrhaging manpower losses.

Ludendorff's Certainty Disappears into a Dark Hole

Worse, as the whole German offensive effort was systematically torn apart, Ludendorff's nerve was unravelling too. The ghost of Helmuth von Moltke[16] and the disaster on the Marne in September 1914 stalked Ludendorff. The promise of victory was dashed then by poor German planning and leadership as well as the unexpected ferocity of the French and British resistance. Now, almost four years later, the stage was now set for a repeat performance: only this time Ludendorff's planning, leadership and mind were about to be entirely unhinged.

In March 1918, German officers had glibly put money on which of their battalions, regiments or divisions would be first past the post in the 'Hindenburg Stakes' when a German victory was declared. Little under three months on, it was abundantly clear to the German people, as well as the troops, that the stakes were very much higher and that it had been more of a race between Ludendorff's ambition and America, as well as the BEF and French.

Ordinary Germans were finally waking up to the grave error that Ludendorff and Hindenburg had made in goading the sleeping giant across the Atlantic into entering the war. Most realized that America had not only declared war against the Fatherland after persistent provocation by Germany over Mexico and through unrestricted submarine warfare, but that she also meant it. The majority of the German people scoffed at the idea that the US could raise an army that could compete with superior German military prowess, but their eyes would be painfully opened between July and November.

But before Ludendorff had put the final touches to what was to prove to be his final offensive, a small but significant surprise was delivered, fittingly, on 4 July – US Independence Day – on the Somme.

4 July: The Capture of Hamel – A Little Allied Triumph, but an Ominous Sign of What was to Come

Despite the combined French, British and US success in holding the Blücher-Yorck and Gneisenau thrusts, the Aisne and Matz offensives had been a major blow to the French, some of whom had predicted disaster on a daily basis. However, Ludendorff's pursuit of a positive result against the French sector, rather than British, had unfortunate consequences for him.

The French were now rather less critical of the BEF's performance during the Michael, Mars and Georgette offensives in the BEF sector and Haig's reputation was boosted even amongst previously sceptical French commanders. Furthermore, Haig had already realized that the American contribution, alongside that of the BEF with its first-class British, Australian, Canadian and New Zealand Divisions,[17] was already having a psychological – and increasingly physical – effect on German morale.

A small but psychologically important action was executed by the Australian Corps, assisted by a token US assault group, on 4 July – American Independence Day. The plan, devised by the Aussie Corps commander, General Sir John Monash, had the objective of capturing

15 July: Operation Marneschütz

the village of Hamel and ironing out a small salient between Villers-Bretonneux and the River Somme. This limited offensive action was designed to provide a more cohesive line for subsequent operations in order to deprive the German defenders of the observation they enjoyed at this time from the high ground overlooking the Somme valley. Sixty of the new Mark V British fighting tanks, twelve supply tanks, as well as the full mix of all arms, including aircraft, artillery, mortars and machine guns, were to support the assaulting infantry when the attack was launched.

The assault formation, 4th Australian Division, carried out intensive combined training with the tanks, artillery and other supporting arms and assaulted alongside the Mark V tanks under cover of a brilliantly delivered creeping barrage. Four Infantry Companies of the American 33rd Division were assigned to the operation and, despite reservations from their C-in-C, US General 'Black Jack' Pershing, played their part in the Hamel operation. On 4 July the Australian and American assault troops took all their objectives in precisely ninety-three minutes, capturing 1,472 German troops and 171 machine guns at a cost of less than 1,000 casualties.

15 July: Operation Marneschütz – Ludendorff's Last Fling

Despite the ominous signs that were being signalled by a renewed Allied confidence, epitomized by the loss of Hamel, Ludendorff somehow stuck to his belief that a success in the French sector would set up his forces for a final assault on the British in Flanders. But now, even pipe dreams were fading from the minds of most German commanders and staff. Nevertheless, like Don Quixote, Ludendorff determined to finish the business in the south with another tilt at the French windmill. The ironic twist in the tale came when he fixed on an offensive in the Marne sector. To prepare for a major assault by no less than forty-three infantry divisions either side of Reims, 5,000 guns hit the French defences and the German assault troops moved up to their jumping-off positions for this 'final blow'.

The 'Second Battle of the Marne' began on 15 July, but this time there was no glorious early success: rather, it started badly and it soon went rapidly downhill. The French Fourth Army, under General Gouraud, knew of the German plans and carried out a pre-emptive

The German Offensives of 1918

artillery counter-barrage onto the trenches packed with German assault troops before they had a chance to move. When they did attack, they were caught left and right and the offensive was almost over before it began. Any brief success was illusory once more, and *Hauptmann* Rudolf Binding was moved to write of the experience:

> I have lived through the most disheartening day of the whole war [...] Our guns bombarded empty French trenches [...] in little folds of the ground [...] lay their machine-gun posts, like lice in the seams and folds of a garment, to give our attacking force a warm reception.

This time, the Kaiser's optimism on the opening day of the offensive was to be dashed almost within hours, rather than days. On the evening of 15 July, Admiral Georg Müller noted:

> His Majesty drove [...] to an observation post north of Rheims to see the start of the new offensive [...] The attack was launched on a 50-mile [*sic*] front on both sides of Rheims [...] At midday we learned that the attack had been successful all along the line and we had advanced up to 5kms [...] The Kaiser returned at 6.00 p.m. His mood was slightly less ebullient than usual. I have the impression that the day's objectives have not been reached.

The source of the Kaiser's different humour became obvious during the following day (16 July):

> I learn that the offensive in the West has been abandoned on account of the heavy resistance encountered. Advances were made only at isolated parts of the line. His Majesty paid the usual visit to the front. On his return he stated that 15,000 prisoners had been taken, Chalons successfully shelled and that our pilots had done valiant work on the Marne. He did not admit that the offensive had proved a total failure.

The game was up. The German offensive plans were shelved when overtaken by a policy of desperate defence, for on 18 July, General Charles Mangin, commanding the French Tenth Army and aided by the French Sixth Army on his right, launched a massive counterstroke

15 July: Operation Marneschütz

against the western sector of the German salient between the Rivers Marne and Aisne. The 1st and 2nd US Divisions were part of the spearhead of Mangin's devastating surprise attack. Tenth and Sixth Armies were supported by thousands of guns and mortars, fighter and bomber aircraft and 225 tanks, many of which were the faster and more manoeuvrable Renault Light models. Within two days, Ludendorff's hard-pressed, stunned and exhausted troops were driven back over 6 miles and by 6 August, all traces of German progress in July had been erased, as they had by then been forced to abandon Soissons and withdraw to positions behind the Aisne and Vesle rivers. The scale of the disaster is revealed by the German losses: over 168,000 casualties, including 29,000 POWs; 793 guns and almost 2,000 machine guns captured.

Ludendorff's last truly desperate gamble had failed and with fatal consequences.

Back at the Kaiser's Court, Admiral Georg Müller noted on the first day of Mangin's counterstroke (18 July):

> This afternoon His Majesty drove to Avesnes to see Hindenburg and Ludendorff. On his return I heard that our Ninth Army has been outflanked at Villers-Cotterets forest and had had to retreat – and that the division that crossed the Marne [earlier] has had to be withdrawn [...] At the audience in Avesnes, Ludendorff was apparently jumpy and the Kaiser had spoken sharply on the failure of the offensive and the influence it will have at home and abroad.

Numerous German letters, memoirs and diaries later revealed the scale of the German Army's plight and both shock and bitterness of the apparently rapid and depressing reversal of fortunes. Gunner Officer Herbert Sulzbach noted on 21st July:

> The word 'hell' expresses something tender and peaceful compared with what is starting here and now [...] [You] can hardly keep going in this massed [French artillery] fire, you can hardly see anything because of the smoke and you have to keep throwing yourself flat on the ground and cannot understand each time why you have not been hit [...] The French have [now] grown hugely

The German Offensives of 1918

in strength, energy and morale [since the mutinies in 1917] – they have got tough and developed considerable endurance. Our division on the right flank has had to give ground [...] a bitter struggle has set in – a struggle for every scrap of ground [...] The telephone hardly ever works, as the lines keep getting shot through. We receive a few messages by lamp signals too, but one cancels each other out [...] [Our latest] order reads: 'The Army's situation requires every foot of ground to be contested. We must put up a tough defence, regardless of the consequences, until reinforcements arrive.'

Never have such demands been made of our men's strength of character, morale and physical endurance as have been made in the last few days: brought in over long distances in forced marches, in hot weather and without rest, and after the failure of their own offensive on which they embarked with great expectations; now thrown into a defensive battle of gigantic scale; they do their duty, they fight, they keep going.

At the highest level, German leadership and authority unravelled rapidly and recriminations at the top raged almost as violently as the German offensive was being ground to dust by the crushing Allied counter-offensive, as described by Georg Müller:

22 July: This afternoon the Kaiser [visited] Avesnes to hear a report. [At last] he was told the bitter truth [...] Hindenburg admitted total failure. The main reason given: Betrayal of our offensive plans.

The ghosts of the First Battle of the Marne in September 1914 and Germany's failure then had come back to haunt Ludendorff, Hindenburg and the German Army on the offensive.

On 24 July 1918, while the Second Battle of the Marne was still under way, General Foch held a conference at Bonbon Château, near Melun, with Haig, Pétain and Pershing, at which he outlined a plan to clear three railways vital to lateral troop movements across the Western Front. Two were in the Eastern sector of the front; one the Amiens–Paris railway, which was behind the British Fourth Army

15 July: Operation Marneschütz

front. At a second meeting on 26 July, which also included Generals Rawlinson and Debeney, the plan was further discussed. Foch's idea was similar to a suggestion Rawlinson had already made to Haig soon after the Battle of Hamel: to disengage the Paris–Amiens railway and push forward in the direction of Roye. Indeed, Haig had instructed Rawlinson to prepare detailed plans on 17 July.

The operation would be undertaken by the British Fourth Army and the French First Army, the latter coming under British command. They faced the German Second Army under General von der Marwitz, which consisted of fourteen divisions, of which British intelligence reckoned four to be unfit for battle. Haig gave the distant town of Ham as the general objective of the attack.

The overall tactical plan was for an advance to the old Outer Amiens Defence Line (which coincided approximately with the Hangest–Caix–Harbonnieres–Méricourt position), after which units of the Cavalry Corps with fast Whippet tanks would pass through towards the line Roye–Chaulnes. The Canadian Corps was to maintain touch with the French and advance south-westerly; the Australian Corps on their left would move easterly; III Corps on the River Somme valley would advance along it, while their 47th Division would pin down and neutralize German units around Albert.

Another major assault was about to be launched on the Somme, but this time the combined arms and integrated Allied blow would crush German morale and force Ludendorff to predict a very gloomy future.

Ultimately, Ludendorff's offensives had yielded some huge but largely meaningless territorial gains, but the strategic objective of a quick victory failed as soon as Operations Michael and Mars came to grief. Operation Georgette was a tacit acknowledgement that the grand plan was becoming a grand illusion, for Ludendorff and his Staff were forced to scale down the Flanders/Lys offensive before it was launched because of the enormous losses already suffered between 21 March and 5 April.

By the end of July, the German Army on the Western Front was severely depleted, exhausted, and found itself in exposed and vulnerable defensive positions formed where their offensives had failed. Within six months German Army strength had fallen from 5.3 million troops to just over 4 million. The bottom of the German manpower

The German Offensives of 1918

barrel could be scraped no more. The situation was a truly wretched one. OHL (the German High Command) estimated that with the current tempo of operations the army needed 200,000 men *per month* to make good the losses suffered. Even the desperate measure of drawing on the next annual class of eighteen-year-olds would provide only 300,000 recruits for the remainder of the year.

Nemesis

The German Army had suffered very serious losses in its spring campaigns and was now being badly hurt on the Marne. At least 13 per cent of its artillery had been destroyed during July alone, and losses from Allied air raids had also been heavy.

At this time, Allied intelligence reckoned that the enemy had 141 divisions on the Western Front line of which seventy-eight were unfit, plus sixty in reserve (twenty-eight unfit). This compares with the 208 battle-ready divisions the Germans had had on 24 May. In comparison, the Allies had 120 divisions in the front line, with a further fifty-five in reserve. Of these, thirty-nine British divisions were in the front line and twelve in reserve. Seven American divisions were now in the front line and another eleven in reserve. All British divisions were now considered battle-ready again after receiving reinforcements following the battering of the spring months. The Allies had regained numerical advantage.

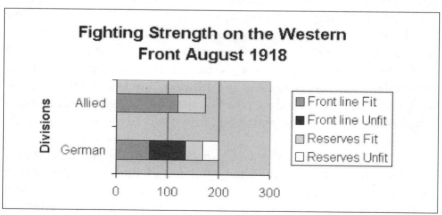

(Source: Chris Baker, *The Long, Long Trail*)

8 August: Amiens

The enemy had also deteriorated in fighting condition: on 1 July 1918, the standard size of a German battalion was cut from 980 to 800 as a result of manpower shortage; 54 per cent of reinforcements they received in the first seven months of 1918 were returned wounded, and 32 per cent were boys of the 1919 class. British artillery by now had achieved tactical dominance over the enemy, through plentiful ammunition and superior counter-battery tactics. In addition, the Royal Air Force had achieved air superiority too. Despite all of this, the enemy remained a formidable opponent.

8 August: Amiens

The first major blow came at Amiens. Henry Rawlinson, in command of Fourth Army, chose to employ nine divisions supported by 400 tanks in the initial assault. Great efforts were made to maintain secrecy, especially in concealing the presence of the Canadian Corps, which had not been involved in fighting for some time. Some Canadian units were sent to Ypres, and Canadian wireless traffic was maintained in Flanders to deceive the enemy.

On 29 July, formal operation orders were issued, which required the line Hangest–Caix–Harbonnieres–Méricourt to be achieved. The French units would operate south of the Amiens–Roye road, the British north. The 5th Australian Division carried out a successful minor operation south of Morlancourt, before the Australian Corps extended 7,000 yards southward, taking over the front that would actually be the start position for the Canadians. The latter arrived in the rear areas by 4 August. The strength of the Fourth Army increased to over 441,000 men. It also had the benefit of the field artillery of the 25th Division and the 5th Canadian Division, and thirteen additional Brigades of heavy artillery. The Tank Corps provided 342 heavy tanks, seventy-two Whippets and 120 supply tanks.

Behind the Fourth Army front, immense preparations were made on the lines of communication, with new railways, dumps, water supplies and many other preparations being made. Labour work would halt at zero and all men be in readiness to move up behind the advance to put roads in a state of repair. Two Casualty Clearing Stations were made available to each corps, and three others for specialist cases made ready,

The German Offensives of 1918

along with ten Ambulance Trains ready to move casualties towards the coast. Prisoner of War cages were also built.

During the nights when the attacking units assembled, German gas shelling was persistent, and on 7 August 25 tanks were destroyed by a heavy enemy bombardment. Soon after dawn on 6 August, a heavy raid on units of the 58th and 18th Divisions near Morlancourt led to a loss of ground 800 yards deep, with some 236 men being taken prisoner. None gave anything away about the imminent attack. Zero Hour was fixed for 4.20 a.m. on 8 August.

The German command received reports of additional noise of movement and even of 100 British tanks seen in the vicinity of Moreuil, but did nothing. On 4 August, Ludendorff said that there was 'nothing to justify this apprehension, provided our troops are vigilant and do their duty'.

The artillery prepared with minimum registration, and laid down a fearsome creeping barrage. The assaulting infantry was deployed in great depth. Leading battalions were arranged in order to advance in five separate waves, 30 yards apart and in particular formations. The leading units stayed as close as possible to the creeping barrage, although the fog and smoke were so thick that in many places men could not see, only hear, the shell explosions. The second, third and fourth moved in single file, in small sections each thirty to sixty yards apart. Machine guns, trench mortars and signals parties went with the fourth wave. At first they would follow tapes, laid out the night before, leading up to less than 300 yards from the front enemy positions. Behind came battalions in larger groups, disposed in a diamond, mopping up stragglers, neutralizing strongpoints and taking prisoners into captivity.

Thick mist in the Avre and Luce valleys assisted the initial advance, but made keeping direction difficult. It cleared in most places by midday.

The Canadian Corps covered the area between the Amiens–Roye road, and the Amiens–Chaulnes railway line. The 3rd Canadian Division on the right, attacking across the ravines of the Luce valley, achieved all objectives by 11 a.m., despite heavy fighting near Hangard cemetery. Only eight out of nineteen of the Mark V tanks of the 5th Battalion, the Tank Corps survived the action. The 1st Canadian

8 August: Amiens

Division on their left captured Aubercourt before being involved in heavy fighting for Hangard Wood. A little further on at Morgemont Wood, the enemy broke and ran.

By 11 a.m. the division was in Cayeux, with eleven of eighteen tanks. The 2nd Canadian Division followed a 'magnificent' barrage and captured Marcelcave with surprising ease, and by 9.20 a.m. was in Wiencourt. Only four of their tanks were lost. By noon the Santerre plateau was quiet, with masses of men and equipment moving forward; the leading infantry were already beyond the cover of their own field artillery. Few German guns were still firing. On the extreme right, the Canadian Cavalry Brigade moved up to cover the flank on the Amiens–Roye road. They captured Beaucourt but ran into resistance at Le Quesnel; other units entered Cayeux Wood, and moved beyond Caix and Guillaucourt. The 4th Canadian Division moved up and passed through the assault units, advancing the line further. By day's end the corps had captured all its objectives with the exception of ground near Le Quesnel.

The Australian Corps covered the area between the Amiens–Chaulnes railway, and the Somme. The 2nd Division attacked on the right, with twenty-three tanks. They advanced into feeble opposition, and had difficulty only as a result of the bad visibility. They reached first objectives by 7.10 a.m., having lost four tanks to mines and direct shell hits. The 3rd Division attacked along the Somme valley, with twenty-four tanks, in very thick fog. Near the river, the 11th Brigade had to move through deep mud, reeds and other undergrowth. The advance could not keep up with the barrage in such conditions, although this risk was negated by good work by the tanks in quelling enemy strongpoints, and in feeble and wild fire by the Germans.

By 7 a.m., the two attacking brigades were on their objective, having captured many hundreds of prisoners and guns. The 5th and 4th Australian Divisions passed through as planned at about 8.20 a.m. By 1.30 a.m. the corps had captured all its objectives, except at the flanks with the neighbouring corps. A strong feature of the second part of the advance was the coordination of infantry and artillery with Cavalry units, tanks and armoured cars. The Royal Air Force also played a large part, especially in harassing retreating German units.

The German Offensives of 1918

That evening, the German plight was poignantly encapsulated by an Aussie soldier, Gunner J.R. Armitage, who was moving forward with his gun battery when he came across a German in a sorry state. He wrote later that:

> I saw a man, and in the bright moonlight, I could see his face. I nearly shot him but, as he seemed to be making very painful progress and was staring down at me as he crawled towards me, I finally went towards him. He let out a croak and called 'Not shoot, not kill me.' When I ventured closer, I found a badly wounded German. He had a leg almost blown off and a bad wound in the side. I got help and we dressed his side but could not do anything about his leg. At first he was certain he was going to be shot. We managed to reassure him [...] he had been wounded in our advance and had lain in a thicket all night afraid to come out until pain forced him to. The morphine we gave him eased his pain a bit and among other things he gratefully forced on me was a 2nd class order of the Iron Cross.

Sadly, the wounded German was eventually killed by his own side, when they bombed an Allied casualty dressing station on the following morning.

To the Australian Corps' left, the British III Corps had the difficult objective of capturing the high ground north of the River Somme in order to cover the flank of the advancing Australians. In terms of distance, this was a more modest objective than those set for south of the river, but the ground was far more complex and difficult, especially for tanks. All divisions of the corps had been heavily depleted during the year, and were now largely composed of young soldiers, with relatively few experienced NCOs and officers. The 58th and 18th Divisions attacked, and despite thick fog and the very recent arrival in position of some of its units, at first advanced easily. By 9.30 a.m. the 58th had captured Sailly Lorette and had an excellent view of Chipilly, 2,500 yards over the next spur. On the left the 18th Division, attacking without the aid of tanks, ran into strong resistance.

On the German side it was 'The Black Day of the German Army,' according to Erich Ludendorff – and it really was the beginning of the

8 August: Amiens

end for Germany. Nine assaulting British and Dominion divisions – the same number of initial assault divisions and on a similar frontage to that of 1 July 1916 – had attacked on the Somme once more. But the difference in results could not have been more marked. Amiens stands even today as a clear and great military victory, which was planned and executed professionally, thoroughly and brilliantly on the day. Yet, today it stands also as an all-but-forgotten achievement. A pragmatic Haig, who had learned so much since the Somme in 1916 and given his army and corps commanders the responsibility for devising and executing the Amiens offensive noted later that:

> Within the space of five days the town of Amiens and the railway centring upon it had been disengaged. Twenty German divisions had been heavily defeated by thirteen British [and Dominion] Infantry and three cavalry divisions, assisted by a regiment of the American 33rd Division and supported by some four hundred tanks. Nearly 22,000 German prisoners and over 400 guns had been taken by us and our line had been pushed forward to a depth of 12 miles in a vital sector.[18]

Admiral Georg Müller, at a silent and depressing Kaiser's headquarters wrote gloomily:

> 8th August: Disastrous news from the Somme. The French, British, Australians and Canadians have broken through our front to a depth of 12km. The Kaiser was in very low spirits this evening.

Then, after the true scale of the disaster was revealed by the third day of the battle, he noted:

> 11th August: His Majesty behaved very calmly yesterday at his meeting with Hindenburg and Ludendorff at Avesnes. No word of reproach, but on the other hand the remark: 'Naturally things can't go on like this indefinitely and we must find a way to end it all.'

The German Offensives of 1918

At the end of the battle on 11 August, the total BEF casualties amounted to just over 22,200 of all ranks, killed, wounded and missing. German losses were a staggering 74,000, of which 50,000 were to be prisoners of war.

'The Hundred Days'

In August, the British, French and American armies mounted a series of rolling attacks that ruptured the German defensive line. It marked the steady Allied progress that was to become known as 'The Hundred Days' to Armistice.

In Germany, Evelyn Blücher recorded in the latter part of the month that:

> Ludendorff has publicly acknowledged the failure of the Great Offensives [...] It seems impossible now for him to force any decisive, successful battle this year. [Still] officers here say that Ludendorff would have been successful if the heavy losses of the Allies had not been speedily made up again. In a single month over 335,000 men were thrown across and every gun and machine gun replaced. It is apparently the unity of command that has restored Allied fortunes [...] and the American Army alone will soon be as big as the German.

Ludendorff's predicament was largely a result of his and the German High Command's own doing. What is particularly relevant in this record from a well-informed, well-educated – and English – woman, who had spent the majority of the war in the German Capital, is what was not acknowledged at that time. The unsustainable losses of the German Army, the impossibility of even the most resourceful German Quartermaster to sustain each of the preceding 'Great Offensives' and especially the curse of Ludendorff's virtually unquestioned yet questionable authority 'in the name of the Kaiser'.

The situation in Germany itself, too, was now desperate. Hunger and disease were everywhere and the Fatherland appeared to have been virtually stripped of any remaining manpower that could have made good the losses that were being so severely felt on the Western Front. Valentine Kühns and his father, who had served at the front

Operation Hagen: The 'Decisive' Offensive That Never Was

Ludendorff believed that he could revisit the failed 'Georgette' Offensive by resuming it, despite the exigencies and limitations imposed by the planning and conduct of the subsequent offensives between May and July 1918. Throughout April, May and June, a number of options for a 'decisive' thrust after Operation Marneschütz-Reims were considered and discussed by Ludendorff, Hindenburg and the Army Group Commanders.

By the end of June, the consensus was for one more major effort in Flanders. By 1 July, a plan was drawn up and preliminary orders issued to prepare for the new offensive. Crown Prince Rupprecht of Bavaria's Group of Armies in the north was to take the leading role.

The plan, graphically illustrated in David T. Zabecki's book examining the 1918 offensives from the operational perspective, shows that the German Sixth Army, commanded by General Ferdinand von Quast, would attack with LV and XIX Korps in the south towards the vital BEF road and rail junction at Hazebrouck. Simultaneously, the German Fourth Army, led by General Friedrich Sixt von Armin, was to launch no less than five corps, (III Bavarian, Guards Reserve, X Reserve, XVIII Reserve and the élite Guards Korps) on a 37km front between Meteren and Boesinghe north of Ypres. The aim was to smash the British Second Army under General Sir Hubert Plumer, break through the Allied (including the Belgian Army in the north) defences and sweep north-west towards the Channel Ports.

Amazingly, even after the disaster that followed the launch of Operation Marneschütz-Reims on 15 July and the Allied counter-stroke three days later, the German High Command maintained some hope that Operation Hagen would take place. Alternative plans, like an offensive on a reduced scale, known as Operation Klein-Hagen, were put forward and actively considered until the end of the first week in August.

With the launch of the brilliant Allied assault at Amiens on 8 August and Ludendorff's 'Black Day', any realistic hope for further German offensive operations such as Operation Hagen were dead and buried.

For a more in-depth analysis of this little-known aspect of the German Offensives, see: David T. Zabecki, *The German 1918 Offensives: A Case Study in the Operational Art of War* (Oxford, Routledge, 2006).

The German Offensives of 1918

throughout 1918, had managed a week's leave at their home town of Thorn. Valentine noted in his diary during this all-too brief a respite:

> Until the 11th of August, Papa and I were there together [...] During the 14 months that I had been away (from Thorn), the boys and girls had grown a head taller. There were so few younger men about [wherever we went]. One sees only invalids, those who are not fit for military service or the poor souls who have been disabled by war. It is only with these men that the girls can flirt as other men are so hard to come by. On my last day of leave, [my friend] Christik is buried. The poor chap died of consumption and was only 20 years old.

September

By September three Allied Army Groups stood poised to strike: The British, in the north, the French in the centre and south and the Americans facing the St Mihiel salient and the Argonne.

The American Army Group's first task as a unified force was to eradicate the German salient, or bulge in the line, at St Mihiel, which they did on 12 September. As one offensive lost its momentum, another would open, giving the Germans no time to reorganize between each Allied assault. The Allied Supremo Ferdinand Foch, ordered 'Everyone to the fight', inspiring the Allies to press on to victory.

Across the Wire

September was a truly dreadful month for the German Army, its commanders and the Kaiser himself. On 2 September it was noted:

> News of further heavy fighting in the West. The English have broken through in strength at Cambrai. This evening Kaiser announced: 'Very grave news from the Army [...] The campaign is lost. Our troops have been retreating since 18 July. We are exhausted. Since [Villers-Cotteret] we have suffered defeat after defeat. Our Army is at the end of its tether.

Across the Wire

The evidence was becoming plainer for the men of the BEF also, despite continued fierce fighting in many places across the front. Brigadier General James Lockhead Jack, DSO, a member of the élite few who had come through the war since 1914 and who had commanded a company, then battalions, prior to his appointment as commander 28th Infantry Brigade (9th Scottish Division), noted in his diary on 20 September that:

A report is to hand that a number of Germans have surrendered to our posts, and that more would have done the same but for the interference of their non-commissioned officers. The enemy's morale must have dipped; one has rarely heard of such a thing happening before an action [in the past].

The majority of the German Army were by now utterly resigned to the prospect of defeat and despair. That they fought on in places with such tenacity and in such good order never ceases to impress and amaze many that either witnessed it then or consider it today. But it was a truly awful experience. Soldiers bemoaned their plight:

Our artillery is fired out [...] We have too few horses. Our fresh troops are anaemic boys in need of rest, who cannot carry a pack, but merely know how to die. By thousands. They understand nothing about warfare, they simply go and let themselves be shot down [...] The summer of 1918 [has been] the most bloody and the most terrible [...] Every man here knows that we are losing the war [...] Still the campaign goes on – the dying goes on.

Some remained as optimistic as they could, although the sense of inevitability had been inculcated even amongst these men. A lifelong friend of Signaller Valentine Kühns, known only as Walter, wrote to him in September from his sector overlooking the River Vesle in retreat after the earlier attacks around Château Thierry:

You have to keep up your courage. The old God still lives. In the terror of the war, my ideals and my literature keep me going.

The German Offensives of 1918

Greetings and a handshake to you! I wonder if we shall ever shake hands again? May God give us the opportunity!

Ludendorff, Hindenburg and an ever weaker Kaiser held on to the reins of power and the German Army simply held on – just. But they all knew that soon 'the war must be ended'. On 28 September, the two military leaders recommended that Germany seek an Armistice with all speed.

In October, as fierce but hopeless fighting continued on the Western Front, the rest of the world sought peace at almost any price. On the 6th, Serbia declared its independence from a terminal Austria-Hungary, as would Czechoslovakia later in the month and on the 7th the Polish leader Marshal Józef Piłsudski announced that the Polish people were asserting their right to self-determination in an independent Poland.

By the final week of October, it was clear that Turkey and Austria-Hungary would find an accommodation and armistice with the Allies and Germany would be officially isolated.

On 17 October it was all but over for the architect of Germany's nemesis: Ludendorff was reported as having a nervous breakdown and rumours were rife across Germany that all was lost – finally; utterly. People talked openly now about Ludendorff's inevitable resignation or removal; about the failure at the front that he and he alone had forced on the Fatherland and about 'mutiny':

The German soldiers, they say, are already turning on their officers and some are throwing hand grenades at them and a train full of officers returning to the front was stopped and all were forced to get out and return home [...] The universal demoralization of the German people is very great and one sometimes has the impression of a flock of sheep who have lost their leader and are going about in a dazed manner looking hopelessly for a loophole of escape from the impending evil.

On 26 October Ludendorff finally 'fell on his sword'. It was a form of 'assisted suicide', but his resistance, his 'fighting spirit' and his dominating manner had all evaporated. He was a broken, disillusioned and bitter man, who scarce believed that any of the disaster that had unfolded for the Fatherland, and now plain for all to see, was his responsibility. It would not be long before he sought – and found – alternative scapegoats.

Aftermath:
A Diabolical
Legacy

The final campaign of the year 1918, known to the Allies as 'The Hundred Days', remains a virtually unrecognized part of the history, the fact and the reality of the First World War. As the decades since 1918 have passed, a year hailed by David Lloyd George at the time as 'the greatest chapter in our military history', the very real and illuminating story of the Allied victory has been lost by increasingly maudlin hindsight about the 'tragedy of the Great War' as a whole.

The reasons for this *volte face* across the years are legion, but perhaps surprisingly, not that complex. Victory was turned into the now long-held view of disillusion and, criminally, the popular view of the 'futility' of it all because after Field Marshal Haig's death in January 1929:

> Lloyd George made it his business to take away all the credit from Field Marshal Haig and his commanders, but in so doing [probably unwittingly] robbed his armies of their just renown. . . . So he tried to pretend that this achievement had not happened; and was supported in this by all those, who for reasons of their own, emotional or doctrinaire saw the Western Front and its generals all villains of history. Such an attitude, of course, chimed

Aftermath: A Diabolical Legacy

well with the post-war disenchantment and pacificism, while journalism is always happier with disaster.[19]

It has always troubled me that Germany's defeat, the utter failure of her offensives under the direction of General Erich Ludendorff and the terrible sacrifice of the German Army have all been played down when compared to the Allied experience of 1918. Historians have written, lectured and presented TV programmes on 1918 that proclaim dramatically that the German Army came within a whisker of an unequivocal triumph in the West and hegemony over Continental Europe. This was simply not the case and Operation Mars proved that Ludendorff's ambition was fanciful at best – and that the Allies would only become stronger as the German Army grew ever weaker in manpower and *matériel*.

On the other hand, by the end of October 1918, when Ludendorff finally left the stage, Germany was on her knees on both the Home and Western Front. The Allies, buoyed by the fact that US military power was beginning to tell and the 'Doughboys' could only grow more confident and adept at overcoming German resistance, anticipated the now inevitable German collapse. Germany was defeated by force-of-arms, fair and square; but circumstances entirely unforeseen and yet profoundly influential then overtook the events that surrounded the Armistice.

Ironically, the Armistice on 11 November 1918 actually boosted German military morale, even if those on the Home Front remained exhausted and merely relieved that the killing had ceased before the German Army was forced to withdraw onto German soil. When a débâcle unfolds there are always scapegoats and excuses and the Armistice provided fertile ground for both. It was not long before rumours spread that the German Army was not only still standing undefeated and undaunted in the field, but also that this heroic struggle and sacrifice had been betrayed by politicians 'back at home' and, in this foment of political change, the betrayal was perpetrated by Communists, Social Democrats and Jews, rather than the military men who had effectively run Germany for much of the war.

To add further 'evidence', many German units were permitted to return to their base garrisons in the Fatherland with their pride intact,

141

The German Offensives of 1918

regimental bands playing and without wholesale incarceration as prisoners of war, as was to happen in May 1945 after the Allies had demanded nothing short of unconditional surrender. In 1918 it was a practical, humane and honourable act by the Allies, but it was, in retrospect, an unfortunate error.

Of equal importance was the influence of the Allied Naval Blockade, although it is often ignored when considering Germany's defeat and its implications post-1918. The Blockade would remain in place until the signing of the Versailles Treaty in the summer of 1919 for perfectly practical reasons, not least of which was to ensure that the remnants of the German Army could not acquire sufficient resources to take the fight to the Allies again in the short-term, as well as put further pressure on Germany to cede to the bruising demands of the Versailles negotiations.

All of these factors were brought into play by the more resentful, petty-minded but influential band of German military men to design, then exploit, the dreadful, insidious myth of 'Die Dolchstoss Theorie' (or 'Stab-in-the-back Theory'). It was nonsense, of course. But circumstances allowed these men, including Ludendorff and Hindenburg, who denied their personal role in Germany's terrible position, to rail against those responsible for the Armistice. They accused the 'politicians' of shameful betrayal behind the backs of the brave men of the German Army who were apparently still fighting to the death in an entirely hopeless cause.

Worse still, the Stab-in-the-back Theory also gave rise to the infamous notion within the fledgling Nazi Party, of which Ludendorff was a key player, that those responsible for the Armistice were nothing more than 'Novemberbrecher' (November criminals). According to Ludendorff, they 'and their kind' deserved nothing less than the contempt of the true German people who had remained steadfast in adversity.

Tragically, honourable defeat led to deep-rooted hatred against Socialism, Communism and Jewish communities and provided evil seeds from which the all-consuming and destructive monster of Nazism would grow, nurtured in its formative years by one Erich Ludendorff.

That monster would then drag Germany into a far bloodier and ruinous conflict than Ludendorff could have ever imagined.

Appendix I:
German Ranks and Equivalents

--------◆(◉)◆--------

German Rank	Command/Equivalent Rank
General Officers	
Generalfeldmarschall	Group of Armies/Field Marshal
Generaloberst	Army/Colonel-General
General der Infanterie/ Kavallerie/ Artillerie	Corps/General of Inf/Cav/Arty
Generalleutnant	Division/Lieutenant-General
Generalmajor	Brigade/Major General
Regimental Officers	
Oberst	Regiment/Colonel
Oberstleutnant	Second-in-Command of Regiment/Lt-Col
Major	Battalion/Major
Hauptmann	Captain – Inf, Arty & Engrs
Rittmeister	Captain – Cav, Air service, Train, (i.e. Logistics units)
Oberleutnant	Lieutenant
Leutnant	Second-Lieutenant
Feldwebelleutnant	Sergeant Major Lieutenant (not commissioned)
Offizierstellvertreter	Acting (Probationary) Officer

The German Offensives of 1918

German Rank	Command/Equivalent Rank
Non-Commissioned Officers (NCOs)	
Fähnrich	Ensign
Oberfeldwebel*	Regimental Sergeant Major (RSM)
Feldwebel*	Coy Sergeant Major (CSM)
Wachtmeister*	Battery/Squadron CSM
Vizefeldwebel*	Colour-Sergeant (Inf, Foot Arty & Engrs)
Vizewachtmeister*	Staff Sergeant (Cav, Field and General Arty & Logistic units)
Sergeant	Sergeant
Unteroffizier	Corporal
Oberjäger	Corporal in Jäger battalion
Obergefreiter	Bombardier (Arty)
Gefreiter	Lance-Bombardier or Lance-Corporal (Inf other arms cf. Arty)
Private Soldiers	
Schütze, Grenadier, Jäger etc.	Private (German title depends on type of Regiment in Inf units)

* All NCOs marked with * were entitled to wear a sash (Portepee) to signify senior NCO rank and were classed as Portepeeträger (literally: 'sash-wearers').

Source: General Staff GHQ BEF, *Handbook of the German Army in War: April 1918* (London/Nashville, IWM/Battery Press).

Appendix II:
Evolution of German
Tactics and Weapons

As early as March 1915 the German War Ministry ordered the formation of a new tactical grouping for special assault purposes, consisting of two × Companies of combat engineers for the use within *Minenwerfer* (mortar) and *Flammenwerfer* (flame-thrower) assault groups. These were supported by an Artillery *Abteilung* (Battery), with four to six × 3.7cm (37mm) guns under the command of Combat Engineer Major Calsow.

From this original concept and 'establishment' evolved the first *Sturm Battailon*, or Storm Battalion, and further experience during the fighting of 1916 led to the establishment of one Storm Battalion per army. The architect of the Storm Battalion was Prussian Guards officer *Hauptmann* Wilhelm 'Willy' Rohr, who led it in its first successful action in retaking the *Hartsmannweiler Kopf* in Alsace in December 1915. Rohr's unit then joined Crown Prince Wilhelm's Fifth Army shortly before the opening of the Verdun offensive in February 1916.

The typical Storm Battalion consisted of two to three infantry assault Companies, one Machine Gun (MG) Company, one *Minenwerfer* (mortar) Company, and an Infantry Gun Battery of four to

The German Offensives of 1918

six × 37mm guns, plus a *Flammenwerfer* Section with four to five flame-throwers.

The number of Storm units was increased to seventeen × battalions by the end of 1916, all as 'Army Troops', but allocated to come under command infantry corps or divisions as the situation demanded. They received their reinforcements from special Ersatz training units based in Germany. However, by the end of 1916, many infantry divisions had inaugurated and utilized their own in-house, or *ad hoc*, 'Storm companies' or 'Storm battalions', although they were not officially recognized by army commands.

The principle of Storm units was that of speed in order to maximise their ability to infiltrate Allied defensive positions, bypass any major strongpoints, and cause mayhem amongst artillery gun lines, rear HQs and communications centres before advancing still further into the enemy Rear Zone, seeking a sector to break through. As a result of this 'need for speed', *Sturmtruppen* were 'lightly equipped, but heavily armed' with rifles, submachine guns and light MGs,[20] as well as sacks of grenades.

This principle of swift-moving, heavily armed assault units was refined and evolved in 1916 with the more formal selection and use of counter-attack units, the *Eingreiftruppen*. *Eingreif* units were formed from battalions within an infantry division. In the latter months of 1916, entire infantry divisions were formally allocated with this task and trained accordingly within each German corps.

The historic reputation of *Sturmtruppen*, particularly at Cambrai in November/December 1917 and during the 1918 offensives, rather clouds the fact that both the use of Storm- and Counter-attack units proved to be both a blessing and a curse. Their more élite status led to the stripping out of the best infantry soldiers, NCOs and officers in many 'Line' infantry battalions for specialist training, so that the parent unit was weakened.

Crown Prince Rupprecht and General Max von Gallwitz, both well-regarded commanders at Army Group level, were concerned about the 'stormtroop problem', which was manifest in the way that they were deployed, aside from the well-known offensives, in more routine defensive or counter-attack/offensive battles. Both believed that the ordinary infantry regiments and battalions were inclined to leave the

Appendix II

'dirty work' to these specialist units and that the high casualty rates amongst these battle-hardened, experienced troops was becoming too high a price to pay. Rupprecht wrote at the time that: 'As instructors of the infantry they were excellent, but the view must not be held that "one cannot attack without them".'

Machine Guns

Even today, the German machine-gunner of 1914–18 has a reputation that far outstrips his British/Dominion or French counterpart, regardless of the fact that in most cases from 1916 onwards, Allied machine-gunners often matched or surpassed those of Fritzie Schmidt.[21] However, as the British/Dominion Machine Gun Corps was being raised in early 1916, German commanders were considering improving the already more plentiful supply of MG teams across the army by providing a reserve of particularly capable MG formations that could be deployed at decisive points.

To this end, OHL ordered the formation of *MG-Scharfschützen Gruppen*, or MG-Marksman Sections, from the best MG teams who had a record as battle-hardened, experienced and supremely able troops. Over 200 of these sections were formed between February and mid-May 1916. With this as the foundation, OHL then introduced a programme through which one in every three MG sections were retrained as MG Marksman Detachments.

This gave the Germans a qualitative and tactical edge in defence throughout 1916 and its legacy was there for all to see in the final months of the war, when local Allied advances were often held up by skilfully deployed stay-behind MG groups or even single gunners.

Also in early 1916, OHL recognized the lack of a German equivalent of the British Lewis Light Machine Gun (LMG). The result was the cumbersome Maxim MG 08/15, which differed from the ubiquitous MG 08 in that it was fitted with a bipod, rather than a tripod, and weighed a few pounds lighter. LMG Detachments were established in July 1916.

Despite his overall record, it is acknowledged that General Erich von Falkenhayn was a true disciple of the importance of the MG. He tripled their numbers in the German Army, produced an MG pool of exceptional combat capability and endorsed the introduction of the

The German Offensives of 1918

German LMG. Ludendorff and von Hindenburg augmented these achievements with a further increase in LMGs and MGs, so that by the end of 1916, a machine-gun section was formally added to every infantry and *Jäger* 'Rifle' Company and the number of LMGs rose from three to six per company. This represented an even more formidable array of 'front-line firepower' in defence.

Artillery

Artillery really came into its own as 1916 progressed and the year proved that the Western Front in particular was a 'war of the guns'. The creeping, or rolling, barrage became a feature of British and French techniques, as well as the latter use of predicted fire. These innovations were eagerly seized on by the German artillery expert, *Oberst* Georg Bruchmüller (later known as 'Durchbruchmüller' or 'Breakthrough-Müller').

In the last two months of 1916 he began to develop a method that would be used brilliantly at Riga in 1917 and then to herald each of the German offensives in 1918. It was the 'hurricane' bombardment, which would be based on predicted fire and last for only three to five hours prior to the main German assault, rather than days.

Appendix III:
ORBATS South to
North on the Morning
of 21 March 1918

Note: British formations, right to left; German formations left to right.

Fifth Army: General Sir Hubert Gough

Fifth Army III Corps
- 58th Division: facing three divisions of Gruppe Gayl north of the Oise
- 18th (Eastern) Division: also facing Gruppe Gayl
- 14th (Light) Division: facing four divisions of the German IV Reserve Korps
- 6th Division: facing elements of the German IV Reserve Korps

Fifth Army XVIII Corps
- 36th (Ulster) Division: facing a fair chunk of grief from elements of the German XVI, IX and III Korps, with a total of fourteen divisions
- 30th Division: facing similar grief to that encountered by 36th Ulsters
- 61st (2nd South Midland) Division: facing same grief as the other two XVIII Corps divisions

The German Offensives of 1918

Fifth Army XIX Corps
- 24th Division: facing attacks from German III, LI and XIV Korps, with nine divisions
- 66th (2nd East Lancs) Division: facing attacks from German III, LI and XIV Korps, with nine divisions

Fifth Army VII Corps
- 16th (Irish) Division: facing elements of ten divisions from the German XIII Reserve Korps/XIII Korps on an 8-mile front
- 21st Division: facing onslaught as 16th (Irish) Division
- 9th (Scottish) Division: as above

Third Army: General Sir Julian Byng
Third Army VI Corps
- 59th (2nd North Midland) Division: facing seven divisions of XVIII and IX Korps
- 34th Division: facing same German Korps as 59th Division
- 3rd Division: facing same as the other two VI Corps divisions

Appendix IV: ORBATS for Operation Georgette

———— ◆(◉)◆ ————

The Battles of the Lys, 9–29 April 1918 and the Battle of Estaires, 9–11 April 1918

First Army
XI Corps
3rd Division, 51st Division, 55th Division, 61st Division, 2nd Brigade of 1st Division, 2nd Portuguese Division and 3rd Brigade of 1st Portuguese Division

XV Corps
29th Division, 31st Division, 34th Division, 40th Division, 50th Division, 74th Brigade of 25th Division

The Battle of Messines, 10–11 April 1918

Second Army
IX Corps
9th (Scottish) Division, 19th Division, 49th Division, 25th Division (less 74th Brigade), 62nd Brigade of 21st Division, 88th Brigade of 29th Division, 100th Brigade of 33rd Division, 102nd Brigade of 34th Division, 108th Brigade of 36th Division

The German Offensives of 1918

The Battle of Hazebrouck, 12–15 April 1918
First Army
I Corps
3rd Division, 4th Division, 55th Division, 3rd Brigade of 1st Division

XI Corps
5th Division, 50th Division, 61st Division

XV Corps
86th and 87th Brigades of 29th Division, 31st Division, 33rd Division, 40th Division, 1st Australian Division, and a Composite Force.

XXII Corps Schools
2nd New Zealand Entrenching Battalion, two Companies of the 18th Battalion, Middlesex Regiment (Pioneers), and XXII Corps Reinforcement Battalion

Note: this action included the Defence of Hinges Ridge, by the 3rd, 4th, 51st and 61st Divisions; and the Defence of Nieppe Forest, by the 5th, 29th, 31st and 1st Australian Divisions.

The Battle of Bailleul, 13–15 April 1918
Second Army
IX Corps
19th Division, 25th Division, 34th Division, 49th Division, 59th Division, 71st Brigade of 6th Division, 88th Brigade of 29th Division, 100th Brigade of 33rd Division, 108th Brigade of 36th Division

XXII Corps
9th (Scottish) Division

The First Battle of Kemmel, 17–19 April 1918
Second Army
IX Corps
19th Division, 25th Division, 33rd Division, 34th Division, 49th Division, 59th Division, 71st Brigade of 6th Division, 88th Brigade of

Appendix IV

29th Division, 89th Brigade of 30th Division, 108th Brigade of 36th Division, Wyatt's Force

Note: Wyatt's Force was hastily formed from various *ad hoc* groups. It was approximately 1,500 strong and led by Brigadier General L. J. Wyatt.

XXII Corps
9th (Scottish) Division, 39th Division, and the 62nd and 64th Brigades of 24th Division

The Battle of Béthune, 18 April 1918

First Army
I Corps
1st Division, 3rd Division, 4th Division

XI Corps
61st Division

The Second Battle of Kemmel, 25–26 April 1918

Second Army
XXII Corps
9th Division, 21st Division, 25th Division (see note on XXXVI Corps), 39th Division, 49th Division, 71st Brigade of 6th Division, 89th Brigade of 30th Division

Plus: Détachement d'Armée du Nord (French)

II Cavalry Corps
3rd Cavalry Division, 28th, 39th and 154th Divisions

XXXVI Corps
2nd Cavalry Division, 34th and 133rd Divisions

Note: The 25th Division were at rest near Proven when the 28th French Division was driven off the summit of Mont Kemmel. They were ordered to assist the French, and were assigned to XXII Corps the next day.

The German Offensives of 1918

The Battle of the Scherpenberg, 29 April 1918
Second Army
XXII Corps
6th Division, 21st Division, 25th Division, 39th Division, 49th Division, South African Brigade of 9th Division, 89th Brigade of 30th Division

Plus: Détachement d'Armée du Nord (French)

II Cavalry Corps
2nd and 3rd Cavalry Divisions, 39th and 154th Divisions

Appendix V: ORBAT for Operation Blücher-Yorck

Note: Operation Blücher-Yorck (27 May to 5 June 1918) was embraced fully by the title 'Blücher-Yorck-Goerz'. The main thrust was Blücher, which was to push on to Château-Thierry and the River Meuse, with smaller flank-supporting drives that were covered by Yorck, around Noyon, on the right and Goerz, around Reims, on the left flanks of the main offensive.

German Seventh Army: General von Boehn

Korps Larisch
5th Division: Attack Division
8th Grenadiers
12th Grenadiers
52nd Infanterie Regiment

6th Division: Attack Division
24th Infanterie Regiment
64th Infanterie Regiment
396th Infanterie Regiment

The German Offensives of 1918

6th Bavarian Reserve Division: Trench Division
25th Bavarian Infanterie Regiment
16th Bavarian Reserve Infanterie Regiment
20th Bavarian Reserve Infanterie Regiment

Korps Wichura
14th Reserve Division: Attack Division
159th Infanterie Regiment
16th Reserve Infanterie Regiment
53rd Reserve Infanterie Regiment

113th Division: Attack Division
36th Fusilier Regiment
66th Infanterie Regiment
27th Infanterie Regiment

37th Division: Attack Division
147th Infanterie Regiment (Marshal von Hindenburg Regiment)
150th Infanterie Regiment
151st Infanterie Regiment

197th Division: Trench Division
273rd Reserve Infanterie Regiment
7th Saxon Jäger Regiment
28th Ersatz Regiment

13th Landwehr Division: Trench Division
15th Landwehr Regiment
60th Landwehr Regiment
82nd Landwehr Regiment

Korps von Winckler
1st Garde Division: Attack Division
1st Foot Garde Regiment
2nd Foot Garde Regiment
3rd Foot Garde Regiment

Appendix V

33rd Division: Attack Division
98th Infanterie Regiment
130th Infanterie Regiment
135th Infanterie Regiment

10th Reserve Division: Attack Division
37th Fusilier Regiment
155th Infanterie Regiment
37th Reserve Infanterie Regiment
442nd Infanterie Regiment
443rd Infanterie Regiment
444th Infanterie Regiment

Korps von Conta
10th Division: Attack Division
6th Grenadier Regiment
47th Infanterie Regiment
398th Infanterie Regiment

28th Division: Attack Division
40th Infanterie Regiment
109th Baden Leib Grenadiers
110th Baden Leib Grenadiers

5th Garde Division: Attack Division
3rd Garde Grenadiers (Queen Elisabeth Regiment)
3rd Foot Garde Regiment
20th Reserve Regiment (3rd Brandenburg)

103rd Division: Trench Division
32nd Infanterie Regiment
71st Infanterie Regiment
144th Infanterie Regiment

36th Division: In Support
Note: only one battalion of the 128th Infanterie Regiment in the line
on 27 May 1918.

The German Offensives of 1918

Korps von Schmettow
50th Division: Attack Division (Westphalia)
39th Fusilier Regiment
53rd Infanterie Regiment
158th Infanterie Regiment

52nd Division: Attack Division (Baden)
111th Infanterie Regiment
169th Infanterie Regiment
170th Infanterie Regiment

7th Reserve Division (Prussian Saxony: Part of Thuringia)
36th Reserve Infanterie Regiment
66th Reserve Infanterie Regiment
72nd Reserve Infanterie Regiment

Appendix VI: ORBAT of French Command on 27 MAY 1918

French Sixth Army – General Denis Auguste Duchêne. The BEF formation caught up in the German offensive here was IX Corps, commanded by General Sir Alexander Hamilton Gordon.

IX Corps Order of Battle

HQ IX Corps & Corps Troops Under Command
8th Division: Major General W. C. G. Heneker
23rd Brigade: Brigadier General W. St G. Grogan VC
2nd Devonshire
2nd West Yorkshire
2nd Middlesex

24th Brigade: Brigadier General R. Haig (wounded)
1st Worcestershire
1st Sherwood Forester
2nd Northamptonshire

The German Offensives of 1918

25th Brigade: Brigadier General R. H. Husey (Killed In Action)
2nd East Lancashire
2nd Royal Berkshire
2nd Rifle Brigade
RFA Brigades: XXXIII, XLV
Field Coys RE: 2, 15, 490
Pioneers: 22nd Durham

21st Division: Major General D. G. M. Campbell
62nd Brigade: Brigadier General G. H. Gater
12/13th Northumberland Fusiliers
1st Lincolnshire
2nd Lincolnshire

64th Brigade: Brigadier General H. R. Headlam
9th KOYLI
15th Durham

110th Brigade: Brigadier General H. R. Cumming
6th Leicestershire
7th Leicestershire
8th Leicestershire
RFA Brigades: XCIV, XCV
Field Coys RE: 97, 98, 126
Pioneers: 14th Northumberland Fusiliers

25th Division: Major General Sir E. G. T. Bainbridge
7th Brigade: Brigadier General C. J. Griffin
10th Cheshire
4th South Staffordshire
1st Wiltshire

74th Brigade: Brigadier General H. M. Craigie Halkett
11th Lancashire Fusiliers
3rd Worcestershire
9th Loyal North Lancashire

Appendix VI

75th Brigade: Brigadier General A. A. Kennedy
11th Cheshire
8th Border Regiment
2nd South Lancashire
RFA Brigades: 110, 112
Field Coys RE: 105, 106, 130
Pioneers: 6th South Wales Borderers

50th Division: Major General H. C. Jackson
149th Brigade: Brigadier General E. P. A. Riddell (wounded)
4th Northumberland Fusiliers
5th Northumberland Fusiliers
6th Northumberland Fusiliers

150th Brigade: Brigadier General H. C. Rees (Prisoner of War)
4th East Yorkshire
4th Yorkshire
5th Yorkshire

151st Brigade: Brigadier General C. T. Martin (Killed in Action)
5th Durham
6th Durham
8th Durham
RFA Brigades: 250th, 251st
Field Coys RE: 7, 446, 447
Pioneers: 7th Durham

Appendix VII:
ORBATS for Operation
Gneisenau

Note: Operation Gneisenau, which drove south via the River Matz towards Compiègne from between Montdidier (west) and Noyon (east), was also supported by a smaller assault south-west of Soissons towards Longpont, which was called Operation Hammerschlag.

German ORBAT

Eighteenth Army: General Oskar Von Hutier
IX Korps (Oetinger)
XVII Korps (Webern)
VIII Korps (Schoeler)
XXXVIII Reserve Korps (Hoffmann)

Seventh Army: General Hans von Boehn
VII Korps (François)
Plus other Korps of Seventh Army for Operation Hammerschlag:
LIV (Larisch)
VIII Reserve (Wichura)

Appendix VII

Allied ORBAT Facing Operation Gneisenau
French Third Army: General Georges Humbert
XXXV Corps
XVIII Corps
V Corps
XXXIII Corps

Appendix VIII: ORBATS for Operation Marneschütz-Reims

Note: The ORBAT shown here lists the German corps attacking on 15 July 1918 and does not include other German corps that were part of the Seventh and First Armies involved, but not taking part at the beginning of the attack.

German ORBAT

Seventh Army: General Hans von Boehn
XXIII Reserve Korps (Kathen)
VIII Reserve Korps (Wichura)
IV Reserve Korps (Conta)
LXV Korps (Schmettow)
VI Reserve (Borne)

First Army: General Bruno Julius von Mudra
VII Reserve Korps (Lindequist)
XIV Korps (Gontard)
XXIV Reserve Korps (Langer)

Appendix VIII

Third Army: General Karl von Einem
XII Korps (Nidda)
I Bavarian Korps (Enders)
XVI Korps (Hohenvorn)

Allied ORBAT Facing Operation Marneschütz-Reims

French Sixth Army: General Jean Degoutte
Two × Corps (not designated)

French Fifth Army: General Mathias Berthelot
Three × Corps (not designated)

French Fourth Army: General Henri Joseph Gouraud
Three × Corps (not designated)

Note: all the data above is based on Vol. 14 of the German Official History of the First World War: Oberkommando des Heeres, *Der Weltkrieg, 1914 bis 1918, Volume 14: Die Kriegsführung an der Westfront im Jahre 1918* (Berlin, Mittler und Sohn, 1944).

Notes

1. BEF = British Expeditionary Force. A term used to identify the British Expeditionary Force sent to France and Belgium to augment the French defences in August 1914, but later epitomized as an all-arms co-operation.
2. ORBAT – Organization for Battle: the Unit or Formation wartime strength.
3. Poilu: 'Hairy one'. The French nickname for the French soldier, derived from the fact that virtually all French troops sported moustaches.
4. Ersatz – substitute; especially foodstuffs, cooking oil, clothing and other retail products.
5. Bethune and most of his men actually survived not only the German offensives, but the war.
6. His battalion was part of 107th Brigade (of the renowned 36th [Ulster] Division), which was flanked by 108th Brigade on its right and 109th Brigade on its left.
7. Edmund de Wind has no known grave and is commemorated on the Pozières Memorial to the Missing.
8. Sadly, Corporal John Sayer died of his wounds on 18 April when still in German captivity, although he was awarded the VC for his part in this action. He is buried at Le Cateau Military Cemetery. Le Verguier was recaptured on 18th September 1918 by the Australian Corps.
9. Evelyn Blücher was married to a descendant of the great Marshal.
10. Marrières Wood: NW of Mont St Quentin near Peronne.

Notes

11. An extract from W. W. 'Skipper' Francis' *Australia Will Be There* – one of the most popular Australian songs of the First World War.
12. He was the late Labour MP & Minister Barbara Cartland's father.
13. 8th Division History, 1914–1918.
14. The 5th Battery (XLV Brigade) was honoured along with the 2nd Devons when cited in French Army Orders for their heroic last-stand and both units were subsequently awarded the Croix de Guerre.
15. DLI – the Durham Light Infantry.
16. Von Moltke had died a totally broken man in 1916.
17. As well as the South African Brigade of 9th Scottish Division and the Newfoundland Regiment.
18. Haig's Despatch, 21st December 1918.
19. Terraine, John, *To Win a War: 1918, the Year of Victory* (London, Sidgwick & Jackson, 1978), pp. 13–14.
20. Bergmann SMG, Maxim 08/15 'light' MG, as well as re-bored British Lewis LMGs, plus the *Stielhandgranate* (Stick grenade, or 'Potato masher') and the smaller, but more accurate and longer-range *Eiergranate* (egg grenade).
21. Fritzie Schmidt – i.e. the German equivalent of 'Tommy Atkins'.

Bibliography

Bundesarchiv and German Archive Sources

Bayerischen Kriegsarchiv, *Die Bayern im grossen Kriege, 1914–1918* (München, Verlag des Bayerischen Kriegsarchiv, 1928)

Reichsarchiv, *Der Weltkrieg, 1914–1918*, Zwölfter Band: *Die Kriegführung im Frühjahr 1917* (Volume 12: *The Conduct of the War in early 1917*) (Berlin, E. S. Mittler und Sohn, 1939)

Reichsarchiv, *Der Weltkrieg, 1914–1918*, Dreizehnter Band: *Die Kriegführung im Sommer und Herbst 1917 – Die Ereignisse ausserhalb der Westfront bis November 1917* (Volume 13: *The Conduct of the War in Summer and Autumn 1917 and the Events beyond the Western Front (In other theatres of war) until November 1917*) (Berlin, E. S. Mittler und Sohn, 1942)

Reichsarchiv, *Der Weltkrieg, 1914–1918*, Vierzehnter Band: *Die Kriegführung an der Westfront im Jahre 1918* (Volume 14: *The Conduct of the War on the Western Front in 1918*) (Berlin, E. S. Mittler und Sohn, 1944)

'Regt. No.' – German Regimental Histories: Erinnerungs-blätter deutscher Regimenter (Oldenburg, Gerhard Stalling, Various 1918–1930s)

Berger, G., *Die 204te Infanterie Division im Weltkrieg 1914–1918* (Stuttgart, Bellser Verlag, 1922)

Beumelburg, Walter, *Flandern 1917: Schlachten des Weltkrieges* (Oldenburg, Stallung, 1928)

Lossberg, Gen Fritz von, *Mein Tätigkeit im Weltkriege, 1914–1918* (Berlin, E. S. Mittler und Sohn, 1922)

Bibliography

Printed Books and Articles: German Source Material

Benöhr, Obergefreiter Franz, *Recollections, Memoirs of Service with Intelligence Branch of Imperial German HQ (OHL) 1917–1918* (courtesy of the Liddle Collection)

Binding, Rudolf, *Aus dem Kriege* (translated as *A Fatalist at War*, London, George Allen & Unwin, 1929)

Blücher, Evelyn Princess, *An English Wife in Berlin: A Private Memoir of Events, Politics and Daily Life in Germany throughout the War and the Social Revolution in 1918* (New York, E. P. Dutton & Company, 1920)

Cron, Hermann, *Geschischte des Deutschen Heeres im Weltkriege, 1914–1918* (Berlin, Siegesmund, 1937 and translated/republished version)

Cron, Hermann, *Imperial German Army, 1914–1918; Organization, Structure, Orders of Battle* (Solihull, Helion & Company, 2002)

Einem, General H. von, *Ein Armee Führer erlebt den Weltkrieg* (Leipzig, 1938)

Gallwitz, *General Max von, Erleben im Westen 1916–1918* (Berlin, E. S. Mittler und Sohn, 1928)

Görlitz, Walter, *Deutsche Generalstab 1657–1945* (*A History of the German General Staff*, translated by Brian Battershaw, New York, Praeger, 1953)

Hindenburg, Feld-Marshal Paul von Mecklenburg und von (translated by F. A. Holt), *Out of My Life* (London, New York, Toronto and Melbourne, Cassell and Company, 1920)

Hoffmann, Rudolf, *Der Deutsche Soldat – Briefe aus dem Weltkrieg* (München, Albert Langen/Georg Müller, 1937). GHI Ref: Sf. 11/117

Jünger, Ernst, *In Stahlgewittern* (*Storm of Steel*, first published Berlin, E. S. Mittler und Sohn, 1920)

Kabisch, Michael, *Die Grosse Schlacht in Frankreich im Lenz 1918* (Berlin, Schlegel, 1921)

Kühl, General Hermann von, *Der Weltkrieg 1914–1918*, Vols. I & II (Berlin, Kolk, 1928, translation by Colonel Roderick Macleod DSO, MC, RA)

Kühl, General Hermann von, *Entstehung, Durchführung und Zusammenbruch der Offensive von 1918* (Berlin, Deutsche Verlag, 1921)

The German Offensives of 1918

Kühns, Edwin Valentine (Trans: Joyce Kühns), *The Diary of a Young German Soldier, 1917–1918* (London, Avon Books, 1998. Also held as pre-published MSS in IWM Department of Documents, Ref: 97/4/1)

Ludendorff, General Erich, *My War Memories, 1914–1918: Volume I, 1914–1916* (London, Hutchinson & Co, 1919)

Ludendorff, General Erich, *My War Memories, 1914–1918: Volume II, 1917–1918* (London, Hutchinson & Co, 1919)

Moser, Gen-Lt Otto von, *Die Württemberger in Weltkriege 1914–1918* (Württemberg Official History, Stuttgart, Bellsen Verlag, 1925)

Müller, Admiral Georg von, *Regierte der Kaiser?* (Göttingen, Frankfurt, Berlin, Munsterschmidt-Verlag, 1949. Also translated and published as: *The Kaiser and His Court: The First World War Diaries of Admiral Georg von Müller*, London, Macdonald, 1961)

Rupprecht of Bavaria, Crown Prince, *In Treuefest: Mein Kriegstagebuch* (*My War Diary*, München, Deutsche National Verlag, 1928)

Schubert-Weller, Christoph, *Kein Schönrer Tod: Die Militarisierung der männlichen Jugend und ihr Einsatz im Ersten Weltkrieg, 1890–1918* (*No finer Death: the militarisation of Young Men and their Experience of the First World War, 1890–1918*, Weinheim und München, Juventa Verlag, 1998. GHI Ref: Sf. 10/140)

Stratz, Rudolf, Der Weltkrieg, *Ein deutsches Volksbuch von dem Weltgeschehen 1914 bis 1918* (*A People's Book on World Events of 1914–1918*, Berlin, Verlag Scherl, 1933)

Sulzbach, Herbert, *Zwei lebende Mauern* (published in 1935, later translated by Richard Thonger and published as *With the German Guns: Four Years on the Western Front*, London, Leo Cooper, 1973/1998)

Tschuppik, Karl, Ludendorff, *die Tragödie des Fachmanns* (published Vienna, 1930, later translated by W. H. Johnston and published in English as: *Ludendorff, The Tragedy of a Specialist*, London, George Allen & Unwin Ltd, 1932)

Zuckmayer, Carl, *Der Teufels General* (*The Devil's General*, Berlin, E. S. Mittler, 1946)

Bibliography

Imperial War Museum

Department of Documents: Tactical Pamphlets/Captured and Translated

German Documents

SS135: Instructions for the Training of Infantry Divisions for Offensive Action, August 1917/Revised April 1918 and The Division in the Attack, November 1918

SS143: Platoon Training (Evolving Tactics), 1916–1918

SS151: Notes and Information from Captured Enemy (German) Documents, March 1917 to August 1918

SS356: Handbook of the German Army in War: January 1917/April 1918 and November 1918

SS555: Vocabulary of German Military Terms and Abbreviations; First Edition 1917, Second Edition 1918

SS567: Diagram Showing Organization of a German Regimental Defensive Sector: 18th July 1918

SS574: The Construction of German Defensive Positions, 18th August 1918

SS600: Organization of the Infantry Battalion and Normal Formation for the Attack: April 1917

SS703: Manual of Position Warfare for All Arms, Special Part: The Experience Gained During the English and French Offensives in Spring to October 1917

SS710, BEF GHQ (November 1917): Translation of Pamphlet/ Instructions on new German Tactics (Brauchitsch), dated 11th November 1917

SS712, BEF GHQ, November 1917: Extracts No. 12 from German Documents and Correspondence: Conditions at the front and Military Morale (25 November 1917)

SS735: BEF GHQ, Translations of Captured German Documents, February to September 1918

SS745/SS745(2), BEF GHQ, Description of the Siegfried Line – September 1918 (German Second Army)

SS753, BEF GHQ (Intelligence): Change in Discipline and Morale of the German Army, January to September 1918 (7 September 1918)

The German Offensives of 1918

Other German Documents on 1918: SS737, SS742, SS754, SS757, SS778, SS787

References CDS 1–20: German Military Engineering, Mines and Trench Warfare; March 1917–November 1918

German Miscellaneous 13 (Ger Misc 7 [13]): Brigade and Regimental War Diaries and Records 1916–1918

Military Documents/Papers

Air Ministry (A.I.2.) *Handbook of German Military and Naval Aviation (War), 1914–1918, October 1918* (London, IWM/Battery Press, Impression, 1995)

American Expeditionary Force (AEF), General Staff, Intelligence Section, *Histories of 251 Divisions of the German Army, which participated in the War (1914–1918)* (Washington, USAF HQ, 1919)

Bruchmüller, Oberst Georg, *Die Artillerie beim Angriff im Stellungskrieg* (Berlin, E. S. Mittler und Sohn, 1926)

Gehre, L., *Die Deutsche Kraftverteilung während des Weltkriegs* (Berlin, E. S. Mittler und Sohn, 1914–1919): German Strengths in Divisions on 15th and last days of every month of the War (comparing 'Strength Returns' of BEF/French forces)

General Staff (Intelligence) BEF, translations of primary German Tactical/Doctrine documents:

    a. 'The Attack in Position Warfare, 1st January 1918' (BEF issue Oct 1918)

    b. 'The Principles of Command in the Defensive Battle in Position Warfare, 1st March 1917' (BEF issue, May 1917)

    c. 'The Principles of Command in the Defensive Battle in Position Warfare, 1st September 1917, with amendments on 7th July and 8th August 1918' (Translation of text October 1918)

General Staff, War Office, *The German Forces in the Field, 7th Revision, 11th November 1918* (London, IWM/Battery Press, Impression, 1995)

General Staff (Intelligence), *Vocabulary of German Military Terms and Abbreviations, 2nd Edition, July 1918* (London, IWM/Battery Press, Impression, 1995)

172

Bibliography

General Staff (GS BEF), *Handbook of the German Army in War, April 1918* (London, IWM/Battery Press, Impression, 1996)

Kerbey, John, '1918 – Year of Victory' (*Army Quarterly and Defence Journal*, Vol. 129, No.2, July 1999, pp. 290–295)

Wynne, G. C., *The Development of the German Defensive Battle in 1917 and its Influence on British Defensive Tactics* (Army Quarterly, Vol. 34, April 1937)

Printed Books and Articles

Official Histories

Bean, C. E. W., *Official History of Australia in the War of 1914–1918* (Sydney, Angus & Robertson, 1938–1942)

Edmonds, Brig-Gen Sir James E., *The Official History of the War: Military Operations in France and Belgium, 1914–1918* (British Official History [BOH], published by HMSO, 1922–1949)

Jones, H. A., *The War in the Air: Official History of the Great War 1914–1918* (London, HMSO/Hamish Hamilton, 1928/1969)

New Zealand, *The Official History of the New Zealand Effort in the Great War*, Vol. II: *The New Zealanders in France* (Auckland, Whitcombe and Tombs, 1921/1923)

Pétain, Marshal Henri Philippe, *Verdun* (Paris, Payot, 1920)

Books, Articles and Other Sources (General)

Ashworth, Tony, *Trench Warfare, 1914–1918: The Live and Let Live System* (London, Macmillan Press, 1980)

Asprey, Robert, B., *The German High Command at War: Hindenburg and Ludendorff Conduct World War I* (New York, William Morrow & Co., 1991)

Bailey, Jonathan, *The First World War and the Birth of the Modern Style of Warfare* (Camberley, Strategic and Combat Studies Institute, 1996)

Baker, Chris, The Long, Long Trail: Western Front Association website at http://www.1914-1918.net/bat22A.htm

Baring, Maurice, *Flying Corps Headquarters 1914–1918* (London, Buchan & Enright, 1920)

The German Offensives of 1918

Barnett, Correlli, *The Sword Bearers: Studies in Supreme Command in the First World War* (London, Eyre & Spottiswoode, 1963)

Barnett, Correlli, *The Great War* (London, Park Lane Press, 1979 and republished 2003 in association with BBC Re-transmission of 'The Great War' TV Series)

Blaxland, Gregory, *Amiens: 1918* (London, Frederick Müller Ltd, 1968)

Bond, Brian, *War and Society in Europe 1870–1970* (Stroud, Sutton, 1984)

Boraston, J. H. & Bax, C. E. O., *The Eighth Division in War (1914–1919)* (London: Medici Society, 1926)

Bridgewater, Patrick, *The German Poets of the First World War* (London & Sydney, Croom Helm Ltd, 1985). GHI Ref: Sf.11/130

Cecil, Hugh and Liddle, Peter (Ed.), *Facing Armageddon: The First World War Experienced* (London, Leo Cooper, 1996)

Cleaver, Hugh, *Operation Mars: The British Perspective* (Study Paper as part of MA Thesis, 2007)

Cooper, Bryan, *The Ironclads of Cambrai* (London, Souvenir Press, 1967)

Cross, Tim, *The Lost Voices of World War I: An International Anthology of Writers, Poets and Playwrights* (London, Bloomsbury Publishing, 1988)

Dennis, Peter and Grey, Jeffrey, *Defining 1918 Victory* (Canberra, Australian Army History Unit, Australian Defence Force Academy [ADFA], 1999)

Dennis, Peter *et al*, *Oxford Companion to Australian Military History* (Oxford, Melbourne, Auckland, New York, OUP, 1995)

Ellis, John, *Eye Deep in Hell: The Western Front 1914–1918* (London, Croom Helm, 1979)

Evans, Martin Marix, *Retreat, Hell! We Just Got Here! The American Expeditionary Force in France 1917–1918* (Oxford, Osprey Military, 1998)

Everest, J. H., *The First Battle of the Tanks* (London, Arthur H. Stockwell, 1943)

Gibbs, Philip, *Realities of War* (London, William Heinemann, 1920)

Gibot, Jean-Luc and Gorczynski, Philippe (translation by Wendy MacAdam), *Following the Tanks at Cambrai; 20th November– 7th December 1917* (Arras, Imprint, 1999)

Bibliography

Gilbert, Martin, *The First World War* (London, Weidenfeld & Nicholson, 1994)

Gray, Randal, *Kaiserschlacht 1918: The Final German Offensive* (London, Osprey Publishing, 1991)

Griffith, Paddy, *Battle Tactics of the Western Front: The British Army's Art of Attack, 1916–1918* (New Haven and London, Yale University Press, 1994)

Gudmundsson, Bruce I., *Stormtroops Tactic: Innovation in the German Army 1914–1918* (New York, Praeger, 1989)

Haythornthwaite, Philip J., *The World War One Source Book* (London, Cassell, 1992)

Herwig, Holger H., *The First World War: Germany and Austria-Hungary, 1914–1918* (London, Arnold, 1997)

Kitchen, Martin, *The German Offensives of 1918* (Stroud, Tempus Publishing, 2001)

Knight, Jill, *The Civil Service Rifles in the Great War: 'All Bloody Gentlemen'* (Barnsley, Pen & Sword Military, 2004)

Leach, Barry A., *The German General Staff* (London, Ballantine Books, 1990)

Lloyd George, David, *War Memoirs* (London, Nicholson & Watson, 1934)

Lupfer, Timothy T., *The Dynamics of Doctrine: The Change in German Tactical Doctrine During the First World War*, Leavenworth Papers No. 4 (Fort Leavenworth Kansas, U.S. Army Command and General Staff College Combat Studies Institute, 1981)

Macksey, Kenneth, *Why the Germans Lose at War* (London, Greenhill Books, 1996)

Middlebrook, Martin, *The Kaiser's Battle, 21 March 1918, the First Day of the German Spring Offensive* (London, Allen Lane, 1978)

Middlebrook, Martin and Middlebrook, Mary, *The Somme Battlefields, A Comprehensive Guide from Crécy to the Two World Wars* (London, Viking/Penguin Books, 1991/1994)

Moyer, Laurence V., *Victory Must be Ours: Germany in the Great War 1914–1918* (London, Leo Cooper, 1995)

Nash, David, *German Infantry 1914–1918* (London, Altmark, 1971)

Nevin, Thomas, *Ernst Jünger and Germany: Into the Abyss 1914–1945* (London, Constable & Co., 1997)

The German Offensives of 1918

Oldham, Peter, *The Hindenburg Line* (London, Leo Cooper, 1995)

Oldham, Peter, *Messines Ridge, 1914–1918* (London, Leo Cooper, 1998)

Palazzo, Albert, *Seeking Victory on the Western Front: The British Army & Chemical Warfare in World War I* (Lincoln and London, University of Nebraska Press, 2000)

Palmer, Alan, *The Kaiser: Warlord of the Second Reich* London, Weidenfeld and Nicholson (1978)

Parkinson, Roger, *Tormented Warrior: Ludendorff and the Supreme Command* (London, Hodder and Stoughton, 1978)

Paschal, Colonel Rod, *The Defeat of Imperial Germany 1917–1918* (New York, De Capo Press, 1994)

Passingham, Ian, *All the Kaiser's Men: The Life and Death of the German Army on the Western Front, 1914 to 1918* (Stroud, Sutton Publishing, 2004)

Pershing, General John Joseph, *My Experiences in the World War* (London, Hodder & Stoughton, 1931)

Philpott, William J., *Anglo-French Relations and Strategy on the Western Front, 1914 to1918* (London/New York, Macmillan, 1996)

Pitt, Barrie, *1918 The Last Act* (London, Cassell, 1962)

Remarque, Erich Maria, *All Quiet on the Western Front* (London, Putman & Co, 1929)

Rogerson, Sidney, *The Last of the Ebb* (London, Arthur Baker, 1937)

Samuels, Martin, *Doctrine and Dogma: German and British Infantry Tactics in the First World War* (New York, Greenwood, 1992)

Samuels, Martin, *Command or Control? Command, Training and Tactics in the British and German Armies, 1888–1918* (London, Frank Cass, 1996)

Sheffield, Gary, *Forgotten Victory: The First World War, Myths and Realities* (London, Headline, 2001)

Simkins, Peter, *Chronicles of the Great War: The Western Front, 1914–1918* (Godalming, CLB International and Bramley Books, 1991 & 1997)

Spears, Sir Edward, *Prelude to Victory* (London, Cape, 1939)

Steel, Nigel and Hart, Peter, *Tumult in the Clouds: The British Experience of the War in the Air, 1914–1918* (London, Hodder & Stoughton, 1997)

Bibliography

Swinton, Maj-Gen Ernest, *Twenty Years After* (London, Amalgamated Press, 1938)

Terraine, John, *Douglas Haig, the Educated Soldier* (London, Hutchinson, 1963)

Terraine, John, *General Jack's Diary: War on the Western Front 1914–1918* (London, Cassell & Co, 1964)

Terraine, John, *The Western Front, 1914–1918* (London, Hutchinson & Co., 1964)

Terraine, John, *The Smoke and the Fire: Myths and Anti-Myths of War 1861–1945* (London, Sidgwick & Jackson, 1980)

Terraine, John, *White Heat: The New Warfare 1914–1918* (London, Guild Publishing, 1982)

Terraine, John, *To Win a War: 1918, The Year of Victory* (London, Macmillan, 1986)

Van der Kiste, John, *Kaiser Wilhelm II: Germany's Last Emperor* (Stroud, Sutton Publishing, 1999/2001)

Van Emden, Richard, *Prisoners of the Kaiser: The Last POWs of the Great War* (Barnsley, Pen & Sword, 2000)

Wheeler-Bennett, Sir John, *Hindenburg: The Wooden Titan* (London, Macmillan, 1967)

Wrigley, Chris J., *Lloyd George* (Oxford, Blackwell Publishers, 1992)

Zabeki, David T., *The German 1918 Offensives: A Case Study in the Operational Level of War* (London & New York, Routledge Class Series: Strategy and History, 2006)

Public Record Office, Kew; Principal References

CAB 23: War Cabinet Minutes

WO95: Operational War Diaries

WO106: Directorate of Military Operations Files

WO153: Artillery Operational Maps and Operation Orders

WO158: Operations, BEF

WO256: Field Marshal Sir Douglas Haig: Diaries/Records, including copies of captured German orders/documents

Index

Index

The German Offensives of 1918

Index